W9-ARV-705

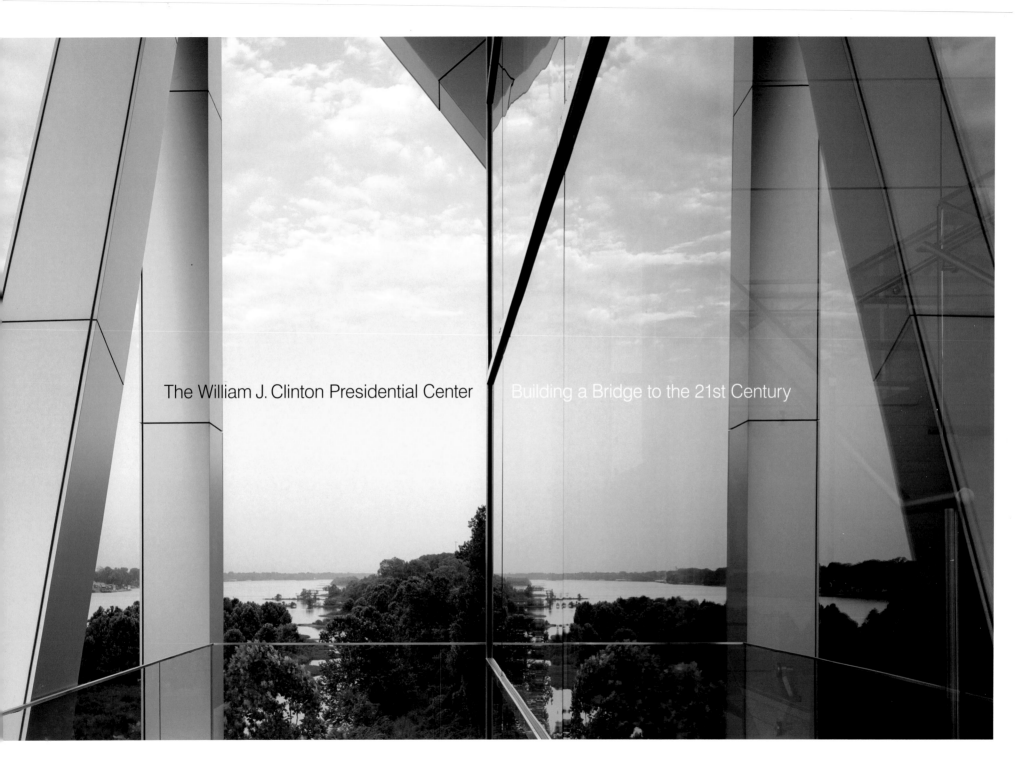

The William J. Clinton Presidential Center   Building a Bridge to the 21st Century

© 2006 by RAA Editions

Published by RAA Editions
88 Pine Street
New York NY 10005
www.raany.com

ISBN-13: 978-0-9789-8680-3
ISBN-10: 0-9789-8680-6

All rights reserved. This book
may not be reproduced, in whole
or in part, including illustrations,
in any form (beyond that copying
permitted by Section 107 and 108
of the U.S. Copyright Law and
except by reviewers for the public
press), without written permission
from the publishers.

Photo credits appear on page 168

Printed in Canada

10 9 8 7 6 5 4 3 2 1

THE WILLIAM J. CLINTON PRESIDENTIAL CENTER

BUILDING A BRIDGE TO THE 21st CENTURY

RAA | *Editions*

CONTENTS

"MY GREATEST WISH FOR THIS LIBRARY IS FOR YOUNG PEOPLE TO SEE, NOT WHAT I DID WITH MY LIFE, BUT WHAT THEY CAN DO WITH THEIR LIVES; TO BELIEVE, AS I DO, THAT PUBLIC SERVICE IS A NOBLE CALLING."

—PRESIDENT CLINTON

Portrait of President Clinton by Yousuf Karsh, 1993.

Introduction
Welcome to the Clinton Presidential Center

Welcome to the Clinton Presidential Center. This modern building, arching over the timeless Arkansas River, never fails to fill me with hope. The Center is first and foremost a presidential library, but it is also a museum as well as a place for people to come together to study the issues of today so that we can meet the challenges of tomorrow. If you take a single message from your visit here, I hope it is the same one that motivated the tireless and dedicated people who worked with me through eight exciting years in Washington: Public service is a noble calling, and doing the people's business is a solemn trust.

The American presidency is a unique institution. For many of us, the President is almost as familiar as a member of the family. Every four years when we elect a President, it is as if all of America comes together and sits for a family portrait. It is a picture that tells us very much about how we see ourselves now and how we would like to see ourselves tomorrow.

It was very important to me that this Center be in Arkansas, and especially in Little Rock, where so much of my philosophy of leadership and public service took shape. My years in Arkansas were eventful ones—a time when this quiet corner of the South was thrust into the forefront of the Civil Rights movement and when, as in the rest of America, the economy was transformed by technological changes that profoundly affected the daily life of every family. First as a schoolboy, then as a young man who chose to make a career of public service in my home state, and finally, through five terms as governor, my bedrock political beliefs were formed in Arkansas. It was here that I first asked myself the question that guided me through two terms in the White House and now in the work of the Clinton Foundation and the Clinton School of Public Service. It is a question—and a goal—that every representative of the people must strive to answer: "How can my actions help improve the life of the people I serve and the future of our children?"

As I reflect on this Center, I find myself thinking how much of my life has been enriched by libraries. When Lonnie Lubben, my sophomore English teacher at Hot Springs High piled on the assignments, it was in the school library that I met Shakespeare's characters. From his heroes, villains, and common folk I learned that every human being has a rich and complex story, if we only take the time to seek it out. In those same years, term paper research also led me into the fascinating lives and deeds of the incredibly visionary Americans who created our Constitution. As I studied the thoughts of Jefferson and Madison, Hamilton and Franklin, I learned the power and impact of ideas. I also marveled at how the founding fathers fashioned our Constitution as a framework to bring people of differing points of view together to form a more perfect union. It is a task whose completion will remain always before us.

This Center bears my name, but it is yours as much as it is mine. It tells the story of our recent past so that we all may learn and move forward. In an age when mountains of information are being generated at a constantly accelerating pace, decisions of great consequence are often made more quickly. It has never been more important that we take a breath, and study how we have come to where we are, if we hope to continue to a brighter tomorrow.

I cannot explain the value of such study and reflection any better than Franklin Roosevelt did at the dedication of his library in 1944. He said, "A nation must believe in three things. It must believe in the past. It must believe in the future. It must, above all, believe in the capacity of its own people so to learn from the past that they can gain in judgment in creating their own future."

All that I have learned about the bridge we are all building to that future is in this Center. May it help to instruct you, as it did me, and may you write the next chapters in the great story that is America.

Bill Clinton

A view across the Arkansas River from the Museum.

THE CLINTON CENTER

AN AMERICAN PLACE

As you look westward from the Great Hall of the William J. Clinton Presidential Library, the view of the Arkansas River takes in the six bridges for which Little Rock is known. The Clinton Center is, in a sense, a seventh bridge. As the events of the Clinton Presidency are here woven into the enduring historical fabric of our nation, the ongoing legacy of Bill Clinton remains a work in progress—a bridge to the 21st century.

President Clinton participated in every aspect of the planning for this Center. He resolved early that if the work of a democratic government is doing the people's business, then we, the people, have the right to know how our elected representatives have gone about fulfilling their mission. For that reason, no effort has been spared to ensure that the holdings of this library, the exhibits in the museum are "transparent"—in other words, accessible to all. The 80 million pages

of documents, two million photographs, 13 thousand videotapes, 83 thousand artifacts, and 20 million e-mails ("two of them by me," President Clinton wryly observed at the dedication ceremony) are part of America's heritage, and they rightly belong to every American.

In addition to being a national institution, this Center is playing an important role in the transformation of Little Rock. The energy

"I believe the job of a president is to understand and explain the time in which he serves, to set forth a vision of where we need to go and a strategy of how to get there, and then to pursue it with all his mind and heart. What this Center is to me is the symbol of not only what I tried to do, but what I want to do with the rest of my life—building bridges from yesterday to tomorrow, across racial and religious and ethnic and income and political divides."

—PRESIDENT CLINTON

President Clinton at the ground breaking, December 5, 2001, with dignitaries and key project advocates: Skip Rutherford, Dean Kumpuris, and Bruce Moore.

and vitality that it brings to a nearly abandoned stretch of riverfront has helped to advance the renewal of Little Rock that began in the 1990s. The landscaped grounds accent the architecture of the buildings, but just as important to the planners of the Center, they are a public park for all to enjoy. The vista of the Arkansas River and the high bluffs on the horizon provides an inspiring view of heartland America.

There are four main parts to the William J. Clinton Presidential Center. First and foremost, it is, like all of the presidential libraries, a branch of the National Archives. It serves as the keeper of records for the eventful years when the nation marked the transition from an industrial age to the Information Age.

This is the eleventh presidential library in a nationwide system that preserves the heritage and ongoing work of the American presidency from the era of Herbert Hoover through the two terms of the Clinton Administration. The collection is larger— in sheer numbers of items—than the combined collections of all the libraries from FDR through Ronald Reagan. Its holdings range from Bill Clinton's grade-school essays to his handwritten corrections of his State of the Union speeches to a photo of his joyous first meeting with Nelson Mandela.

Although the Center exists principally to house the presidential archives, 90 percent of visitors come to view the exhibits in the Museum. These exhibits tell the inside story of the Clinton Presidency as lived by the President and his advisers. They provide a direct connection to history through actual memos and rough drafts, up-close photography, video clips, and countless

main entrance to the William J. Clinton Presidential Library.

"I believe our mission in this new century is clear. For good or ill, we live in an interdependent world. Therefore, we have to spend our lives building a global community and an American community of shared responsibilities, shared values, shared benefits. What should our shared values be? Everybody counts. Everybody deserves a chance. Everybody's got a responsibility to fulfill. Our differences do matter, but our common humanity matters more."

—PRESIDENT CLINTON

unique artifacts. The story they tell is one of hard work, long hours, and a shared dedication never to lose focus on the work of the American people.

Whether you study the exhibits in great detail or just tour the Center in an hour or two, you will see the story of the building of an economy that afforded all Americans the most extended period of prosperity in our history. You will ponder the challenge of ancient enmities that continue to threaten the world, and you will take stock of the breathtaking rise of new technologies that give us the ability to respond to future challenges by bringing all nations more closely together into one global community.

As one of our nation's youngest ex-presidents, Bill Clinton intended that this Center be much more than a testament to the past.

It is also a place to take on the tasks of the future, playing an ongoing role in a story yet to be written. Fittingly, the headquarters for engaging the 21st-century future is the nearby 19th-century red brick building—formerly a railroad station named for the Native American Choctaws who lived in Arkansas. It is home to the Clinton Foundation and the Clinton School of Public Service. As part of the University of Arkansas, the school is the first in the nation to offer the degree of Master of Public Service. Here, President Clinton, along with government leaders and policy makers, regularly holds seminars and delivers lectures to a competitively selected group of civic-minded students who—as part of their curriculum—participate in service projects all over the world.

Also located in the Choctaw Building, the offices of the Clinton Foundation serve as a

nerve center for the public service projects and initiatives to which President Clinton and like-minded citizens are devoting their energies. On a project-by-project basis, they are focused on the global challenges of public health, economic opportunity, and racial and religious reconciliation. Through the School and the Foundation, President Clinton continues to pursue his lifelong mission of service and, most importantly, to inspire others to do the same.

The Clinton Global Initiative is a non-partisan catalyst for action, bringing together a community of global leaders to devise and implement innovative solutions to some of the world's most pressing challenges. Here, President Clinton attends the Initiative's first meeting.

THE SITE

The Clinton Center at sunset, within its 30-acre park
on the banks of the Arkansas River.

The landscaped grounds of the park are planted with over
700 trees that represent the region's native flora.

THE SITE
A HOMETOWN PARK FOR A NATIONAL INSTITUTION

Like the city of Little Rock, the Clinton Center is defined by its relationship to the Arkansas River at its door. More than 1,400 miles in length, this waterway is the longest tributary in the whole Mississippi drainage system. In the same way that the river knits the heartland of America together—from the Rockies, to the Great Plains, to the Mississippi Delta—the grounds of the Center are part of a larger effort to create a greenway that reconnects Little Rock to its ancient waterway.

Nearly 30 acres in size, the park surrounding the Center is a major addition to public space in Little Rock. Much of the land for the Center had long been neglected and was largely inaccessible because of a 50-foot bluff that separated the river from the rest of the site. Now that steep drop-off has been graded so that sweeping terraced lawns and gardens go all the way to the water's edge. There is a 2,000-foot promenade that winds through the grounds along the whole length of the

park. A walk from one end to the other reveals constantly changing views of the architecture of the Center. The cantilevered museum appears to soar toward the river and the nation beyond.

Approaching the Center from the revitalized River Market District, President Clinton Avenue is flanked by 75 lacebark elms that will one day form an arching canopy linking the Center to the city. Clinton Avenue

"It was important that the grounds serve as a place where families could come and enjoy the green space. The President wanted a park that would attract the local community as well as visitors to the museum. To have the chance to transform an area from a neglected industrial wasteland to a vibrant park is the kind of thing that makes a landscape architect want to get up in the morning and the President and First Lady were with us 100 percent."

—GEORGE HARGREAVES, LANDSCAPE ARCHITECT

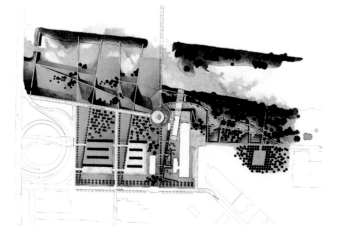

terminates in a wide plaza known as Celebration Circle. Thousands of the paving stones for this dramatic entryway to the Presidential Center bear the names of citizens whose contributions helped to construct the new Center. And in a use that was not planned, but which gratifies everyone associated with the Center, more than a few proposals of marriage have been made at Celebration Circle.

The hills and lawns have been planted with an "Arkansas forest" reflecting the rich biodiversity of this state. Most of the trees, shrubs, and flowers represent the native plants of the Ozarks, the Mississippi Delta, the Gulf, and the Ouachita Mountains. Ash, maple, willow, and oak are among the 700 trees—comprising nearly 30 species— that the landscaping team of Hargreaves Associates incorporated into their master

plan. During the construction of the project, President and Mrs. Clinton expressed their hope that as these areas grow and mature, they will be used by families for picnics and community barbecues—events that remain among Bill Clinton's fondest memories of his boyhood in the Arkansas of the 1950s and 60s.

At the northwestern edge of the Center, a wetland and pond lie off the main channel of the river. You can often see egrets and herons, turtles and bullfrogs, as well as the ducks and geese that migrate each spring and autumn along the Mississippi flyway.

Between the Library and the red brick Choctaw Building there is a "Scholar's Garden." It serves as a quiet refuge from the activity in the surrounding buildings, providing a restful view from the main research rooms. All through the warm months, it is filled with the flowers of

An early sketch of the Clinton Center park by the landscape architect.

ckwise: A walkway between the Choctaw Building and the Scholars'
den; Celebration Circle at main entrance to the Library; Scholars' Garden
bining the Archives; park grounds east of the Library.

such perennial plants as goldflame spiraea, daylily, purple coneflower, sage, and iris.

The grounds to the east of the building are less developed, but they, too, are open to the public. The re-naturalized riverbank here is beginning to look much as it did in the days when the Choctaws netted fish in the river and hunted for game on the woody grasslands beyond. Farther in from the river, a grove of Southern magnolias surrounds a semi-secluded lawn that is well suited to quiet contemplation.

Taken in sum, the grounds, the boldly modern library, the historic Choctaw Building, and the industrial-age Rock Island Railroad Bridge fulfill a national role in preserving the legacy of the Clinton Presidency. At the same time, they play an important part in the everyday life of an American city.

Top: The Choctaw Route train station and the future grounds of the Clinton Center in the late 1950s. Bottom: Aerial view of the site and building under construction in 2003 with downtown Little Rock in the background.

...sculptured landscape of the Clinton Center connects
...e revitalized River Market entertainment district.

THE BUILDING

At dusk, the interior of the museum is revealed through the translucent skin of the Library.
On the third floor the glowing outline of the Oval Office replica is visible.

Specially formulated glass allows natural light to flood the
building while protecting its precious contents.

THE BUILDING REACHING OUT TOWARDS THE FUTURE

The story of how this Center came to be is, like the story of the presidency, a tale of dreams transformed into a practical reality. It is an evolving narrative of wood and stone, steel and glass, all designed to preserve and give access to the huge array of documents and artifacts collected during the two terms of the Clinton Administration.

Well before he left office, President Clinton began to lay the conceptual foundations for a presidential center that could properly fulfill these tasks. He felt that the Center should be a symbol of our heritage, a record of our past, and a jumping-off point for the future. Although no one realized it in the beginning, there was already a powerfully symbolic idea waiting to be recognized. It just took a little while to discover it. At first, President Clinton and the architectural team of James Polshek and Richard Olcott envisioned a building that faced the river.

Many of the earlier designs called for a building that would create a dominating presence on the riverscape.

Then, as more ideas were put forward and discarded, the President and the architects realized that the most striking feature of Little Rock is the six bridges over the Arkansas River. At that point, the simple concept of turning the building 90 degrees took shape. The idea of a bridgelike building was a

"The challenge was to make a building that feels open and light and at the same time is very full of precious artifacts that need to be protected from damaging light. Also from the very first meeting the President made it clear he wanted the building to be "green": as progressive and sustainable as possible and that the journey through it, the play of light, the feel of the materials, the river views should leave you exhilarated."

—JAMES S. POLSHEK AND RICHARD M. OLCOTT, MUSEUM ARCHITECTS

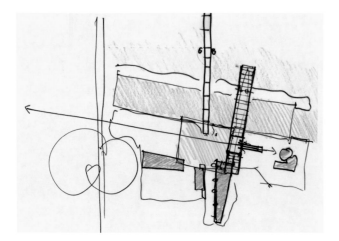

natural extension of the river view with its many spans. Just as important, it was an extension of the President's ideas about this nation. The unmistakable similarity of the Library and Museum to the nearby Rock Island Railroad Bridge invokes a tangible physical link between yesterday and tomorrow: on the one hand, a relic of the 19th century and, on the other, a major architectural statement of the 21st century that looks as if it is reaching out toward the other shore–and the future.

Any building—whether a home or school, factory or church—is experienced in two ways. Our first encounter is with the outside—the interaction of building and landscape. But far more of our experience takes place once we are inside. In this regard, the impression a building makes is the sum of many things. How do we fit into the space? How does the play of light open up a space and lead us to

one thing or another? How do the materials used evoke memories and emotions?

The architects had to keep all of this in mind while designing a building that would fulfill its primary purposes. First, as a part of the National Archives, this Center has a vital mission, mandated by Congress, to preserve and protect the artifacts and documents of the Clinton Presidency for future generations of scholars, students, citizens, and visitors from all over the world. Much of that work takes place behind the scenes, in storage facilities at the southern end of the main building.

The second requirement is that the Center provide a memorable experience for the great majority of visitors, who come not to consult the Archives but to see the public spaces—the Museum, Great Hall, and

The play of light and shadow changes the building's appearance and color throughout the day.

The Clinton Library under construction in late 2002. The building—
which is supported on the ground in only three places—took over five
years and over 1,500 people to plan and build.

Head-on view of the cantilevered
north section of the building.

"A derelict slice of urban turf has been given new social purpose. A landscape has been created to provide a bold and satisfying setting for architecture. And, in addition to being a model of environmental responsiveness, the architecture greatly enlivens its surroundings."

—BENJAMIN FORGEY, THE WASHINGTON POST

other multi-purpose spaces that are used for art exhibitions, concerts, lectures, and various other events.

Among the first things that visitors comment on is the natural light that fills the building. The main entry hall is literally defined by the light pouring through the vast expanses of glass on the east and west sides of the building. The sheer amount of light cannot help but lift the spirit, but it also is potentially damaging to the irreplaceable artifacts and documents on display. A long search and much experimentation led to a special type of glass that lets in the greatest amount of light with little effect on the contents of the museum.

Apart from its esthetic value, natural light also helped the architects to meet another of President Clinton's goals for this Center:

It had to be as environmentally responsible as possible. In recognition of having met that goal, the Clinton Presidential Center became the first presidential library to receive a silver rating for "Leadership in Energy and Environmental Design" (abbreviated as LEED).

By using recycled tires, bottles, and cans in many aspects of construction, the architects employed the cast-offs of the 20th century to create a shining example of environmental responsibility in the 21st century. The main building uses 34 percent less energy than a conventional building, partly because it makes use of direct and passive solar energy. And the addition of trees and green space on the 30-acre site, where previously there were paved streets and warehouses, has effectively reduced runoff into the Arkansas River by 23 percent. When new materials were called for, the preferred source was always regional,

so that the 20 tons of stone are Tennessee marble and limestone instead of the imported marble often used for public buildings. Finally, wherever possible, the choice was made to use renewable resources.

This Center serves a number of purposes. It is a symbol of renewal for the city of Little Rock. It is an example of architecture and urban planning that embodies the future while preserving our past and for this it received the American Institute of Architecture's highest award in 2006. But at its core, it is a place to reflect upon the meaning of the presidency and its role in the life of every citizen.

...itors at the Clinton Library's main entrance.

THE MUSEUM

View down the main exhibit hall towards the Arkansas River.
Its 18 columns hold over five thousand archive boxes, used to store
a small percentage of the Clinton Administration's documents.

Visitors study an exhibit case in the Museum.

THE MUSEUM
A BRIEF HISTORY OF THE CLINTON YEARS

Through the careful attention that he brought to everything he undertook, Bill Clinton gave the exhibits in this Presidential Center the unique benefit of what you might call a "curator in chief." More than any other account of his administration, this museum presents a comprehensive portrait of President Clinton as he saw his life and times.

Historians may rightfully pick and choose their themes as they try to explain the eight eventful, prosperous, exciting, and peaceful years of the Clinton Presidency. Likewise, journalists, by the nature of their profession, may give us the sound bites and headlines of the day, often informed with the political passions of the moment. But President Clinton felt that, in planning the exhibits in this Museum, he had an opportunity to share his singular perspective with scholars and schoolchildren, citizens of this country, and citizens of the world.

The key question, of course, is how to begin to tell the adventure of leading the world's greatest democratic enterprise and to do so in all of its depth. The short answer is that the task can never be completed. The longer answer is to offer as much as space and time will allow and then leave it to the visitor to choose any of a number of paths through the material. There is a model for this kind of repository of knowledge: It is one that collects the broadest range of material and information and displays it in an

"President Clinton said that he wanted his library to tell the first substantive history of his administration—including many unpublished stories and often overlooked accomplishments. He and his former White House staff were involved from the beginning to the end of the project and they always brought their perspective, knowledge, and enthusiasm for the work that they did."

—RALPH APPELBAUM AND MELANIE IDE, MUSEUM DESIGNERS

easily accessible arrangement where each visitor can delve into it according to his or her level of interest. It is called a library. Using a library as the organizing concept of the main exhibit room at the Center had special meaning for Bill Clinton. As a young man, he was one of the few Americans chosen each year for a Rhodes Scholarship to Oxford University. During that time he took the opportunity to visit some of the historic buildings of Europe. Among them, the soaring reading room (called The Long Room) of the library at Trinity College in Dublin made a lasting impression. At the suggestion of the museum's designers, that graceful yet imposing cathedral of learning was used as a model for the exhibit space dealing with the work of the Clinton Administration.

The literal, and symbolic, backbone of the main exhibit hall is a freestanding Timeline that contains the complete presidential schedules of almost 3,000 days of the administration. Its panels recount the major events of the Clinton years and places them in the context of his presidency. Iconic photographs from all areas of life—ranging from sports to music to natural disasters, scientific breakthroughs, and military conflict—give a graphic frame of reference to the personalities, events and issues of the time during which the Clinton Administration embodied the hopes and carried the burdens of the nation.

A series of 28-foot columns defines two major areas of thematically organized exhibit alcoves. These towering columns also serve as bookshelves for almost 5,000 archival boxes that hold nearly eight percent of the actual historical documents of the administration. The alcoves, arranged on both sides of the hall, present an in-depth look at the way in

overview: The Timeline runs down the center of the main floor with the
icy Alcoves on either side, and the Mezzanine holds personal mementos
he family and artifacts from the White House years.

"Once people look at the sheer amount of things that the administration tackled, the common reaction is that they are amazed. They begin to think about the presidency and its tremendous scope. Whatever their politics, folks can't help but feel the energy in this place."

—BOB GEE, MUSEUM VOLUNTEER

which the President addressed the major issues of the times. From the initiatives that produced the longest period of economic prosperity in our history, to the continuing question of adequate health care for all Americans, to the threat of terrorism, to the ever more partisan struggles in our political life, to the implications of global warming, to the safety of our streets and the soundness of our children's education—these alcoves remind us of the tasks that history laid upon this last administration of the millennium and how President Clinton's team came at every problem with focus and a plan for the future.

Through their words and papers, through their deeds, through photographs and documents, videos and sound recordings, the President and his closest advisors have here presented the raw materials of the history they helped make. Like a building that takes shape brick

by brick, the record of his administration is the sum of the events, great and small, that Bill Clinton pondered and then acted upon. If there is one thing that he hoped to convey through this mass of material it is that, for eight years, through good times and bad, he began each year with a blueprint outlined in the State of the Union address, and he came to work every day and unwaveringly attempted to build upon that plan.

Though the work of the presidency is clearly the heart of the exhibits, the personal story of the President and his family is well represented. It is told through exhibits that range from Cub Scout merit badges to saxophones, Christmas trees to the priceless table settings for a formal White House dinner. The great humor that was always a hallmark of the Clinton style is recounted on video, and a grand case displays some of

the beautiful gifts that the Clintons accepted on behalf of the American people when world leaders visited the White House.

Typically, every visitor's last stop at the Museum is the only full-size replica of a place that truly symbolizes the American presidency: the Oval Office. As for almost everyone who steps foot in it, being in the Oval Office always gave Bill Clinton a feeling of standing on democracy's hallowed ground. For many of us this replica is as close as we will ever get to the Oval Office. For that reason, Bill Clinton wanted each and every visitor to this Center to feel the majesty and the mystique of this cornerstone of our republic. Flooded with natural light, this replica, like its true-life counterpart, never fails to suggest the sense of possibility, optimism, and determination to make tomorrow better than today that are the enduring hallmarks of America's 42nd president.

ew of the Campaign exhibit (below) and the
-size replica of the Oval Office (above).

Visitors studying the Campaign exhibit are reflected in a photo
of the President taken on election night, 1992.

A CAMPAIGN FOR THE FUTURE

Democratic presidential hopeful Bill Clinton is silhouetted
against the U.S. flag at a rally in New Hampshire.

Bill Clinton was elected to the presidency in 1992, a time of economic distress, social division, and a deep yearning for change and hope.

Seasoned observers had said that President George H. W. Bush was unbeatable. In 1991, when Governor Clinton decided to run for the White House, Bush had popular approval ratings near 90 percent. But Bill Clinton wasn't listening to the pundits. He was listening to the people he met on his travels across the country— hardworking Americans facing economic hardship, and poor people who had been left behind. They all felt forgotten by the people in power.

In the primaries that followed, Clinton defeated five other contenders for the nomination of the Democratic party. In the general election, he faced not only the incumbent President, but also the independent Ross Perot, a tough-talking Texas businessman. But it was Bill Clinton who claimed the mantle as the candidate of change, the only candidate with a clear vision for America's future, and the ideas and political will to make it reality.

On election night, Clinton received 370 electoral votes to Bush's 168. The man from Hope won 33 states— and the presidency of the United States.

upporter in an enthusiastic crowd in Madison, sconsin holds an Elvis poster. President Clinton was lknamed Elvis by the press.

Bill Clinton waves to supporters from the steps of the Clinton-Gore campaign bus. The bus tours allowed the candidates to meet people all across America.

Buttons from the 1992 presidential campaign, selected from President Clinton's personal collection.

Top to bottom: The Clintons and Gores on the campaign bus in North Carolina; the candidate works the crowd; center stage at the Democatic Convention to accept the party nomination.

Top: Practicing "Heartbreak Hotel" before appearing on the Arsenio Hall show, Santa Monica, California. Bottom: The Clintons relax backstage in Milwaukee.

The Clintons are cheered in a Chicago hotel after the big win on Super Tuesday. Reflecting on the campaign Bill Clinton said, "The last two weeks have been like a ride on the Coney Island Cyclone. Now that I've been through it, I've got to admit I've had a ball."

"THERE IS NOTHING WRONG WITH AMERICA THAT CANNOT BE CURED BY WHAT IS RIGHT WITH AMERICA.

AND SO TODAY, WE PLEDGE TO END AN ERA OF DEADLOCK AND DRIFT— A NEW SEASON OF AMERICAN RENEWAL HAS BEGUN.

TO RENEW AMERICA, WE MUST BE BOLD."

—PRESIDENT CLINTON, FIRST INAUGURAL ADDRESS, JANUARY 20, 1993

President Clinton at the Old State House in Little Rock on election night, 1992.

President Clinton takes the oath of office at his first inauguration, January 20, 1993.

THE INAUGURATIO

THE CLINTON CABINET

President Clinton used the Cabinet Room for critical meetings, such as discussing economic strategy, planning military operations, developing peace agreements, and discussions with members of Congress. This full-scale recreation features interactive touch screens that let visitors to the museum learn about the role of each member of the administration, investigate how decisions were made, crises averted, and battles won. The tallest chair, bearing a brass plaque marked "The President," sits in a position of honor at the table's center.

Clockwise from left: President Clinton's cabinet in the Cabinet Room, 1993; President Clinton's cabinet on the North Lawn of the White House, 1996; museum visitors in the Cabinet Room.

THE VICE PRESIDENT

Vice President Gore takes the oath
of office on January 20, 1993.

Bill Clinton's selection of Al Gore as his running mate in 1992 marked a generational shift: For the first time, both candidates on a presidential ticket were born after World War II. The pair became the youngest team ever to make it to the White House, and they brought a new vitality to the work of government.

A Vietnam veteran and father of four, Al Gore served eight years in the House of Representatives and eight years in the U.S. Senate—where he became known as an expert on a broad range of issues, from information technology to the environment, and from arms control to Alzheimer's. Empowered by President Clinton to bring that same energy to the White House, Al Gore transformed the vice presidency, turning a largely ceremonial position into a center of ideas and innovation.

From his office in the West Wing, Gore played an important role in nearly every major decision. He took the lead on a number of high-profile issues: shaping environmental policy, guiding U.S.–Russia relations, streamlining the federal government, and leading administration efforts to support the burgeoning information and telecommunications revolution. He embodied Harry S. Truman's description of the vice presidency: "It is the man who makes the office, not the office the man."

Clockwise from top left: Vice President Gore helped connect 95% of U.S. schools to the internet; his Reinventing Government initiative launched a historic effort to make government smaller, smarter, and more effective; Al Gore, here with his Russian counterpart Viktor Chernomyrdin, played a critical role in shaping U.S. foreign policy; greeting workers at a U.S.-funded training project in South Africa.

President Clinton delivers his State of the Union address, February 4, 1997.

A TIMELINE
THE CLINTON ADMINISTRATION
1993-2000

In the fall of 1991, Governor Bill Clinton traveled to Georgetown University—his alma mater—to deliver three speeches on his vision for the future and plans for the presidency. He called this philosophy the "New Covenant." Together, these speeches served as a road map for the nation, marking a "Third Way" between the old dead ends.

Over the next eight years, by acting on the belief that the United States lives in one world and shares one economy, and that the events and decisions made in our country have direct impact on everyday people everywhere, the administration helped restore people's faith that government could be an instrument for the common good. "In 1992 we had a road map," the President said in his 2000 State of the Union address. "Today, we have results."

Timeline highlights the actions and accomplishments of the Clinton [pre]sidency against the background of the events, personalities and issues [th]ose years. Video monitors show President Clinton's annual State of the Union address in which he put forth his blueprint for the year ahead. Interactive screens and binders holding all of the President's daily schedules provide another window into the work of the Clinton Administration.

1993

The excitement that accompanied Bill Clinton's election as America's 42nd President was so great that nearly a million people turned out for Inaugural Day. To a nation grown weary of recession, he spoke of change and declared: "There is nothing wrong with America that can't be cured by what is right with America."

The ideas that led Clinton to campaign as "a different kind of Democrat" became a plan to take America in a new direction. The President's economic proposal reflected his campaign promise to "focus like a laser beam on the economy." Republicans called it a job killer. It passed both houses of Congress without a single Republican vote and went on to create the longest economic expansion in American history. Similarly, the candidate who argued that America must cooperate with other nations in an age of globalization gained bipartisan support as President for the North American Free Trade Agreement between the United States, Canada, and Mexico. He also played an active role in brokering a new

opening toward peace in the Middle East. In 1993, two key campaign promises—the national service program, AmeriCorps; and the Family and Medical Leave Act—became law.

The administration also had some early setbacks: withdrawn cabinet nominations; a controversial move to reverse the ban on gays and lesbians in the military; and a failed rescue mission in Somalia. Nevertheless, Bill Clinton's first year as President proved, as he had argued during the campaign, that government could once again be a force for improving people's lives.

World Trade Center explosion, New York City.

Fighter jets overhead enforcing no-fly zone, Sarajevo.

Branch Davidian compound, Waco, Texas.

Missouri and Mississippi Rivers overflow, creating devastating floods in the Midwest.

Endeavour shuttle releases Hubble Space Telescope.

Hard-line rebels surren Boris Yeltsin's troops re Russian Parliament.

"GIVEN A FAIR CHANCE, I KNOW AMERICAN WORKERS
CAN COMPETE AND WIN IN OUR OWN HEMISPHERE AND
THROUGHOUT THE WORLD. THOSE WHO BELIEVE
OTHERWISE UNDERESTIMATE THE AMERICAN PEOPLE."

—PRESIDENT CLINTON, NOVEMBER 6, 1993

Deficit reduction plan passes
Senate, helps transform a record
deficit to a record surplus.

Family and Medical
Leave Act signed.

Israel and PLO sign peace agreement.

NAFTA is signed, expanding trade
with Mexico and Canada.

Nelson Mandela and F. W. de Klerk of South
Africa receive the Nobel Peace Prize.

1994

The sweeping changes that would define the 1990s took shape in the Clinton administration's second year: the growth of the global economy; the spread of new democracies; the tragedy of wars driven by age-old hatreds; and rapid growth of a communication tool that would define a new information age— the Internet.

In Washington, battle lines were drawn around the role of government. The administration believed that America and its government should help shape these developments to benefit everyone, while a Republican minority argued that government itself was the problem. The administration believed that America should be a leading force for peace and prosperity in the world, while Congressional Republicans called for America to retreat from the world.

The administration prevailed. In Europe, the President proposed a new vision for security in the post–Cold War world. Efforts to support democracy in Russia, bring peace to Northern Ireland and the Middle East, and liberate the people of Haiti emphasized America's role as a catalyst for positive change. In Congress, the administration successfully signed into law landmark bills on education and crime— but a bill to provide health insurance for all Americans was defeated by negative advertising and charges of "big government."

In the election of 1994, Republicans capitalized on the failure of that health plan and gained control of Congress. While divided government would remain a fact of life for the remainder of the decade, President Clinton worked hard to establish bipartisan cooperation and to move the country forward.

Earthquake, Los Angeles, California.

Running to avoid sniper fire, Sarajevo.

Listening to Nelson Mandela speak during election campaign, South Africa.

Funeral of Jacqueline Kennedy Onassis, New York City.

Rwandan refugees carrying water back world's largest refugee camp, Tanzania.

"WE MUST RETURN TO THE PRINCIPLE THAT IF WE GIVE ORDINARY PEOPLE EQUAL OPPORTUNITY, QUALITY EDUCATION AND A FAIR SHOT AT THE AMERICAN DREAM, THEY WILL DO EXTRAORDINARY THINGS."

—PRESIDENT CLINTON, JANUARY 25, 1994

ay four of the major-league
aseball strike.

Goals 2000 Education
Standards enacted.

Crime bill signed; during the next eight
years, crime rates dropped dramatically.

The administration assembles a
multi-national force to restore Haiti's
democratically-elected government.

General Agreement on Tariffs
and Trade signed by 117 nations,
reducing tariffs and quotas.

Yasser Arafat, Shimon Peres,
and Yitzhak Rabin receive
the Nobel Peace Prize.

1995

The Republican sweep of Congress led some to call Clinton's administration a "failed presidency." Yet one year later, he held a significant lead over his Republican rival for President. How the "comeback kid" became the "comeback President" is the story of 1995.

In April, an anti-government American extremist bombed the Alfred P. Murrah Federal Building in Oklahoma City, killing 168 victims. In his eulogy, President Clinton wondered if such tragedy was where government-bashing could lead. In June, the President proposed a balanced budget. That summer, as partisan conflict grew, he delivered three speeches calling on Americans to find common ground. By fall, the President dominated international headlines. He signed the Dayton Peace Accords, which ended the war in Bosnia; attended the funeral of the assassinated Israeli prime minister, Yitzhak Rabin; and received a hero's welcome in Ireland, where he led efforts to sign a peace agreement. At the end

of 1995, the differences over the role of government culminated in a battle over budget priorities. Congressional Republicans demanded drastic cuts to Medicare, Medicaid, education, and the environment. President Clinton disagreed, insisting on a balanced budget that reflected the nation's established values. When the President held firm, Republicans shut down the federal government—twice. But Americans rallied to Bill Clinton's more hopeful vision, marking a turning point in the Clinton Presidency.

Earthquake, Kobe, Japan.

Timothy McVeigh, a suspect in the bombing of Oklahoma City's Federal Building.

Space shuttle Atlantis docked with Russian space station Mir.

O. J. Simpson murder trial, Los Angeles.

Funeral of Israeli prime minister Yitzhak Rabin, Jerusalem.

Returning to find her ho in ruins, Chechnya.

> "ALL AMERICANS HAVE NOT JUST THE RIGHT, BUT A SOLID RESPONSIBILITY, TO RISE AS FAR AS THEIR GOD-GIVEN TALENTS AND DETERMINATION CAN TAKE THEM; AND TO GIVE SOMETHING BACK TO THEIR COMMUNITIES AND THEIR COUNTRY IN RETURN."

—PRESIDENT CLINTON, JANUARY 24, 1995

U.S. loans to Mexico prevent economic collapse.

President Clinton presents balanced budget.

In Beijing, First Lady speaks out on human rights.

Dayton Peace Accords signed, ending brutal conflict in Bosnia.

Republican attempt to enact radical budget leads to two government shutdowns.

1996

By 1996, the nation was regaining its self-confidence. Clinton's economic strategy had helped create eight million new jobs, and a wide majority of Americans believed their nation was headed in the right direction.

In his State of the Union address, the President declared: "The era of big government is over—yet we cannot go back to the time when our citizens were left to fend for themselves."

Unlike 1995, 1996 was marked by legislative achievement. The President partnered with the Congress to end the outdated welfare system; and with Democrats, to raise the minimum wage, allow people to take health insurance from job to job, and protect children from tobacco. With Vice President Gore, he gained bipartisan support to create the V-Chip and a television ratings system, helping parents protect their children from exposure to violence. While critics derided such measures, America's families welcomed them.

At the same time, American cooperation with other nations intensified. The administration worked with Russia to reduce the threat of nuclear weapons,

strengthened military alliances in Japan and South Korea, and saw the first American peacekeepers welcomed in Bosnia.

All this set the stage for a remarkable presidential election year. Republicans nominated Kansas senator Bob Dole, a hero of World War II, who identified himself as a bridge to the past. The President argued that America needed to build a bridge to the 21st century. On November 5, 1996, Bill Clinton became the first Democrat in half a century to be elected to a second term.

Memorial for U.S. Air Force members slain in a truck bombing in Saudi Arabia.

Unabomber is captured in Helena, Montana.

Russian president Boris Yeltsin dances at a rock concert, Rostov, Russia.

TWA Flight 800 explodes over Atlantic, off Long Island.

Suspicious fire at Matthews-Murkland Presbyterian Church, Charlotte, North Carolina.

"EACH OF US MUST HOLD HIGH THE TORCH OF CITIZENSHIP
IN OUR OWN LIVES. NONE OF US CAN FINISH THE RACE ALONE.
WE CAN ONLY ACHIEVE OUR DESTINY TOGETHER—ONE HAND,
ONE GENERATION, ONE AMERICAN CONNECTING TO ANOTHER."

—PRESIDENT CLINTON, JANUARY 23, 1996

Flags fly at half-staff following explosion in Centennial Olympic Park, Atlanta.

The President partners with Democrats in Congress to raise the minimum wage.

Telecommunications Act signed with an electronic pen.

Welfare reform made welfare a second chance instead of a way of life.

Comprehensive Test Ban Treaty signed.

Villagers try to escape the fighting area near Dokan, northern Iraq.

1997

America entered 1997 more peaceful and more prosperous than it had been in a generation. The contentious debate between those who saw government as the problem and those who believed government could be part of the solution had given way to more bipartisan cooperation, culminating in an agreement to balance the federal budget, for the first time in a generation.

Abroad, a new and more interdependent world was rapidly evolving, presenting both opportunities and risks. In North America, the United States cooperated with Mexico to combat drugs and organized crime. The administration supported the Chemical Weapons Convention to keep weapons of mass destruction out of terrorist hands, and worked with the Russian Federation to mutually reduce both nations' nuclear arsenals. The North Atlantic Treaty Organization invited three former satellites of the Soviet Union—Poland, Hungary, and the Czech Republic—to join. When the collapse of Thailand's currency touched off a financial crisis across Asia and threatened economies around the world, President Clinton and

Asian leaders worked together to help calm the crisis. At home, the President initiated a campaign for higher academic standards and opened a national dialogue on race. In Little Rock, Arkansas, 40 years after nine African-Americans met with jeers as they tried to integrate Central High School, they walked through those same doors, held open this time by the President of the United States. Helping all Americans to see our nation as One America remained a driving force for the entirety of Bill Clinton's presidency.

Britain's new Prime Minister, Tony Blair, waves to well-wishers, London.

Fashion designer Gianni Versace murdered in Miami.

Celebrating Hong Kong's return to Chinese sovereignty, Beijing.

Soufrière Hills volcano erupts on Montserrat, British West Indies.

Rover Sojourner on Mars.

Funeral of Diana, Princess of Wales, Lond

"AMERICA IS FAR MORE THAN A PLACE. IT IS AN IDEA,
THE MOST POWERFUL IDEA IN THE HISTORY OF NATIONS....
WE ARE NOW THE BEARERS OF THAT IDEA, LEADING
A GREAT PEOPLE INTO A NEW WORLD."

—PRESIDENT CLINTON, FEBRUARY 4, 1997

Chemical Weapons Convention, limiting the use of chemical weapons in war, ratified by Senate.

Agreement signed allowing Russia to participate in NATO affairs.

President signs Balanced Budget Act.

President Clinton worked with leaders in Asia to calm the financial crisis there.

Waiting for funeral procession of Mother Teresa, Calcutta.

1998

Nineteen ninety-eight was the most eventful year in American politics in a generation. After six years of the Clinton economic strategy, a budget surplus was projected for the first time since 1969. A debate began: what should be done with it? President Clinton gave a four-word answer: save Social Security first.

Abroad, millions of Africans turned out to hear President Clinton speak in the first tour by an American president of sub-Saharan Africa. In Communist China, he spoke about freedom. In Northern Ireland, an American-brokered peace accord ended decades of violence. And in Geneva, the President articulated a vision for a new international trading system. When U.S. embassies in Kenya and Tanzania were bombed, America struck back at the terrorist network of Osama bin Laden. In Iraq, American and British forces used airpower to thwart Saddam Hussein's capacity to build weapons of mass destruction. And when the Middle East peace process was threatened, the President invited Israelis and Palestinians to the

Wye River Plantation, restoring the path toward peace. It was also a year when the President acknowledged making a serious mistake in his personal life, misleading both his family and the country. Adversaries, who opposed his policy agenda, used his personal failing to try to destroy his presidency, culminating in the second impeachment in American history. Yet like every other politically motivated investigation of the President, it led nowhere. The Senate eventually voted to acquit the President.

The lasting impression of 1998 was of America as a leading force for peace and prosperity in the world.

Fidel Castro greets Pope John Paul II after historic mass, Havana, Cuba.

Martin McGuinness and Gerry Adams in approval of historic Belfast accord, Northern Ireland.

Legendary singer Frank Sinatra dies, Los Angeles.

Terrorist bombs explode U.S. embassies in Kenyan and Tanzanian capitals.

Matthew Shepard, a gay college student, was fatally beaten and tied to fence, Laramie, Wyoming.

"WE HAVE MOVED PAST THE STERILE DEBATE BETWEEN THOSE WHO SAY GOVERNMENT IS THE ENEMY AND THOSE WHO SAY GOVERNMENT IS THE ANSWER. MY FELLOW AMERICANS, WE HAVE FOUND A THIRD WAY."

—PRESIDENT CLINTON, JANUARY 27, 1998

President vows to save Social Security.

Good Friday Agreement signed in Northern Ireland.

President begins historic tour of Africa that emphasized the expansion of democracy.

White House announces $70 billion budget surplus.

Hurricane Mitch whirls through Honduras, Central America.

1999

By 1999, the United States had achieved the longest peacetime expansion in its history, and seemed to be the nation best positioned to benefit from globalization. Believing that America's success in the 21st century would depend on the success of other countries, the Clinton Administration led a global effort to expand prosperity to the places left behind, both at home and abroad.

President Clinton proposed to nearly quadruple debt relief for heavily indebted poor countries, if they agreed to spend the savings on reducing poverty and educating their people. He also led a global initiative to pay for vaccines that could help eliminate deadly diseases like AIDS.

The President expanded opportunity at home as well, with a New Markets initiative, bringing jobs and investment to poor rural areas, inner cities, and American Indian reservations. With the help of Vice President Gore, 95 percent of American schools were wired to the Internet by the end of the administration. In the spring, Serbia's President, Slobodan Milosevic, launched a brutal campaign against Muslims in

the Serbian province of Kosovo. President Clinton, determined to avoid another bloody war in the Balkans, urged NATO to intervene. After 78 days of air strikes, Milosevic withdrew his forces. A year later, the Serbian people would overthrow Milosevic in a democratic revolution.

At year's end, Bill Clinton became the first U.S. president to receive the prestigious Charlemagne Prize, for America's role in creating a Europe that was democratic, undivided, and at peace for the first time in history.

Refugees, Kosovo.

Columbine High School massacre, Littleton, Colorado.

John F. Kennedy Jr., his wife, and sister-in-law are killed when his plane crashes off Martha's Vineyard.

Earthquake, Adapazari, Turkey.

Peacekeeping troops in East Timor during independence crisis.

> "NO ONE ANYWHERE IN THE WORLD CAN DOUBT THE ENDURING RESOLVE AND BOUNDLESS CAPACITY OF THE AMERICAN PEOPLE TO WORK TOWARD THAT "MORE PERFECT UNION" OF OUR FOUNDERS' DREAMS."
>
> —PRESIDENT CLINTON, JANUARY 19, 1999

President Clinton fulfilled his commitment to add 100,000 police officers.

President Clinton helped convince the International Labor Organization to ban the worst child labor.

President promotes New Markets initiative.

United States and China reduce tariffs, clearing the way for discussions on arms, the environment, and human rights.

World celebrates millennium.

2000

The Clinton Presidency began with the question of whether government could be a force for positive change in people's lives. By 2000, there could be no doubt. Focusing his administration's efforts on empowering Americans and preparing them for a new century, Bill Clinton brought the nation into a period of unparalleled prosperity.

Having inherited a record deficit from his predecessor, the President left a record surplus for his successor. The administration did not rest, however, and continued to look ahead, addressing long-term challenges. It doubled support for after-school programs; enacted the largest increase in Head Start ever; expanded funding for breast and cervical cancer treatment; and led passage of a landmark Lands Legacy Initiative. Overseas, the administration increased trade with Africa and our Caribbean neighbors, helped open Chinese markets to U.S. products, and brought China into the World Trade Organization. "Plan Colombia" helped Latin America's oldest democracy fight drug trafficking. President Clinton took trips to India

and Vietnam, inaugurating a new era of cooperation with both nations.

There were some disappointments as well. Lasting peace did not come to the Middle East. The President could not overcome Congressional opposition to provide prescription drug coverage to America's older citizens. But our nation entered the 21st century at peace—more prosperous and more respected in the world than it had ever been. The "different kind of Democrat" had given his best efforts to build a different kind of America.

Pope John Paul II stands at the Western Wall, Jerusalem.

DNA samples for Human Genome Project, M.I.T., Cambridge, Massachusetts.

Air France Concorde crashes at takeoff in Paris, killing all aboard.

The 100th birthday of England's Queen Mother.

U.S.S. Cole explodes while refueling, Yemen.

"WE REMAIN A NEW NATION. AND AS LONG AS OUR DREAMS
OUTWEIGH OUR MEMORIES, AMERICA WILL BE FOREVER YOUNG.
THAT IS OUR DESTINY."

—PRESIDENT CLINTON, JANUARY 27, 2000

New national monuments designated, protecting millions of acres.

President Clinton's years in office were the longest period of growth in American history.

President Clinton visits India, speaks to Parliament, and tours villages where he praises local micro-lending initiatives.

Landmark trade partnerships with African and Caribbean nations.

Permanent, normal trade status for China.

A hanging chad in Broward County, Florida, presidential election.

ONE WORLD

"FOREIGN AND DOMESTIC POLICY ARE INSEPARABLE IN TODAY'S WORLD. IF WE'RE NOT STRONG AT HOME, WE CAN'T LEAD THE WORLD WE'VE DONE SO MUCH TO MAKE. AND IF WE WITHDRAW FROM THE WORLD, IT WILL HURT US ECONOMICALLY AT HOME. WE CAN'T LET THIS FALSE CHOICE BETWEEN DOMESTIC POLICY AND FOREIGN POLICY HURT OUR COUNTRY AND OUR ECONOMY.

IN A DYNAMIC NEW ERA, OUR GOAL IS NOT TO RESIST CHANGE, BUT TO SHAPE IT."

—GOVERNOR CLINTON, "A NEW COVENANT FOR AMERICAN SECURITY,"
GEORGETOWN UNIVERSITY, DECEMBER 12, 1991

Clinton Administration Accomplishments

* Fought for peace in the Middle East

* Ended a decade of repression and ethnic cleansing in Kosovo

* Brokered the Good Friday peace accord in Northern Ireland

* Led diplomatic efforts to end the war and foster democracy in Bosnia

* Restored democratic government in Haiti

* Secured Vietnamese cooperation in accounting for MIAs and normalized relations

* Fought proliferation of weapons by improving controls over Russian fissile materials

* Banned antipersonnel land mines that do not self-destruct and self-deactivate

* Enlarged NATO, integrating Hungary, Poland, the Czech Republic, and southeast Europe

* Developed the nation's first comprehensive counter-terrorism strategy, led by a national coordinator

* Responsible for NAFTA, GATT, and nearly 300 other free and fair trade agreements

* Brokered a landmark agreement for China's entry into the World Trade Organization

* Launched annual summit of APEC leaders to meet on economic and other issues

* Helped rescue Mexico's economy with $20 billion in emergency loans

* Gave debt relief to the world's 32 poorest countries

* Funded two million microenterprise loans to poor countries in Asia, Latin America, and Africa

* Quadrupled U.S. assistance to overseas efforts to fight HIV/AIDS

* Funded efforts to develop vaccines for AIDS, malaria, tuberculosis, and other major disease threats

* Supported the Kyoto Treaty on Global Warming, the International Criminal Court, and the Comprehensive Test Ban treaty

The World 1992-2000: A Statistical Portrait

DEMOCRACY	NUCLEAR WARHEADS	POVERTY	LITERACY	TRADE VOLUME	TECHNOLOGY
Percentage of countries with electoral democracies	Total number: U.S., Russia, U.K., China, France	Number of people living on less than $1 a day	Literacy rate of young people 15–25 years old	World foreign direct investment	Number of new web sites
1992: 53%	1992: 52,972	1990: 1,292 million	1990: 84.2%	1990: $202 billion	1993: 130
2000: 63%	2000: 31,535	2000: 1,169 million	2000: 86.8%	2000: $1.5 trillion	2001: 27,585,719

Sources: Freedom in the World 2003; Bulletin of the Atomic Scientists; World Bank; United Nations Statistics Division; UNAIDS Report on the Global HIV/AIDS Epidemic; U.S. International Trade Commission; Web Growth Summary, Matthew Gray

ONE AMERICA

"WE SIMPLY HAVE TO GO BEYOND THE COMPETING IDEAS OF THE OLD POLITICAL ESTABLISHMENT: BEYOND EVERY MAN FOR HIMSELF ON THE ONE HAND AND SOMETHING FOR NOTHING ON THE OTHER.

TO TURN AMERICA AROUND, WE'VE GOT TO HAVE A NEW APPROACH, FOUNDED ON OUR MOST SACRED PRINCIPLES AS A NATION, WITH A VISION FOR THE FUTURE. WE NEED A NEW COVENANT, A SOLEMN AGREEMENT BETWEEN THE PEOPLE AND THEIR GOVERNMENT, TO PROVIDE OPPORTUNITY FOR EVERYBODY, INSPIRE RESPONSIBILITY THROUGHOUT OUR SOCIETY, AND RESTORE A SENSE OF COMMUNITY TO OUR GREAT NATION."

—GOVERNOR CLINTON, "THE NEW COVENANT: RESPONSIBILITY AND REBUILDING THE AMERICAN COMMUNITY,"
GEORGETOWN UNIVERSITY, OCTOBER 23, 1991

Clinton Administration Accomplishments

* Moved from record deficits to record surplus
* Began paying off the national debt
* Created nearly 23 million jobs
* Fastest and longest real wage growth in over three decades
* Family income reached record highs
* Unemployment was the lowest in over three decades
* Record–high home ownership rates
* Lowest overall poverty and child poverty rates since the 1970s
* Expanded the Earned Income Tax Credit
* Enacted the Family and Medical Leave Act
* Increased the minimum wage
* Enacted the Workforce Investment Act
* Signed the Adoption and Safe Families Act
* Created AmeriCorps
* Responsible for Hope Scholarships and Lifetime Learning tax credits

* Expanded Pell grants and work–study program
* Helped communities hire 100,000 quality teachers
* Lowest crime rates in a generation
* Funding for 100,000 more police on the streets
* Guns denied to more than 700,000 felons, fugitives, and domestic abusers
* Responsible for Assault Weapons ban
* Responsible for Safe Schools/Healthy Students Initiative
* Enacted Violence Against Women Act
* Lowest percentage of Americans on welfare in 32 years
* Doubled child–support collections
* Teen births at the lowest rate on record
* Created 40 empowerment zones
* More than 100 rural and urban Enterprise Communities
* New Markets Initiative
* Individual development accounts
* Enacted Kennedy–Kassebaum Health Insurance Portability and Accountability Act

* State Children's Health Insurance Program
* Expanded health care for women with cancer
* Raised child immunization rates to all-time high
* Extended life of Medicare Trust Fund to 2030
* Extended patient protections in Federal health plans
* Increased funding for tobacco education and control
* Created 11 new national monuments
* Established protection for 60 million acres of roadless areas within national forests
* Enacted stronger Safe Drinking Water Act
* Created the Coral Reef Ecosystem Reserve
* Increased investment in biomedical research
* Enacted Motor Voter law
* Smallest federal civilian workforce in 40 years
* Lowest federal spending as a share of the economy since 1966
* Slowest per capita growth of government spending since the 1950s

United States 1992-2000: A Statistical Portrait

CRIME	EMPLOYMENT	POVERTY	EDUCATION	TECHNOLOGY	HEALTH
Crime rate per 100,000 inhabitants	Total non-farm employment	Percentage of people living below poverty line	People 25 and older who have a bachelor's degree	Homes with computers	Percentage of poor children insured
1992: 5,660.2	1992: 108.3 million	1992: 14.8%	1992: 34.3 million	1993: 22.8%	1992: 64.0%
2000: 4,160.5	2000: 130.8 million	2000: 11.3%	2000: 44.8 million	2000: 51%	2000: 69.1%

Sources: FBI Uniform Crime Reports; U.S. Bureau of Labor Statistics; U.S. Census Bureau; Centers for Disease Control; National Center for Education Statistics; U.S. Department of Commerce; U.S. Census Bureau

Entering the main gallery, visitors can delve into the wealth
of material presented in the Policy Alcoves, which represent
different aspects of the work of the Administration.

IDEAS MATTER THE WORK OF THE CLINTON ADMINISTRATION

When Bill Clinton was elected in 1992, he had already developed a road map
for the future and was set to address the many issues facing the nation.
The President's approach to policymaking involved gathering a broad
range of opinions and expert advice. He and his team would then frame
each issue as a challenge to which they would fashion a response.

The Policy Alcoves allow visitors to delve into the range of issues that the
President and his team dealt with over the course of his administration,
and to learn how they responded—from restoring the economy to welfare
reform, from protecting the earth to making peace. Important documents,
photographs, and video, as well as a variety of historic artifacts create
an in depth look at the work of the Clinton Administration.

Each of the 13 Policy Alcoves presents the issues and challenges that the Clinton
administration faced, how it responded to these challenges, and the results of its
efforts. Filled with artifacts and photos and enlivened by video, the alcoves cover
topics ranging from the economy and education to peacemaking.

Restoring
The Economy

Bill Clinton believed that in the 21st century, more than in any previous era, America's leadership in the world would depend on the strength of its economy at home. To put America's house in order, the President proposed a new, three-part economic strategy: balancing the budget for the first time in a generation; investing in people and technology; and opening new foreign markets for U.S. products.

Over the next eight years, these policies ushered in the longest, strongest economic expansion in American history—creating nearly 23 million new jobs, turning record budget deficits into a record surplus, reducing interest rates, and paying down the national debt. In the 1990s, the rising tide of the U.S. economy lifted all boats: in contrast to previous decades, every income group—the rich, the middle class, and especially the poor—saw their incomes increase. One hundred times more people moved out of poverty in the 1990s than during the economic recovery of the previous decade.

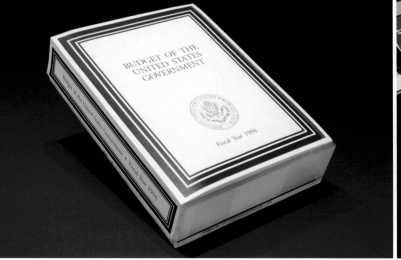

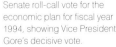

Senate roll-call vote for the economic plan for fiscal year 1994, showing Vice President Gore's decisive vote.

Top to bottom: President Clinton meets with members of his economic team; the signing of the Balanced Budget Act; the budget for fiscal year 1994.

From deficit to record surplus: President Clinton announces milestones in 1993, 1995, 1998, 1999.

"America's success was not a matter of chance; it was a matter of choice." —PRESIDENT CLINTON, 08/14/00

pre-existing condition
LC-140.P

August 12, 1994

President Bill Clinton
c/o Health Care Reform Information Center
The White House
Washington, D.C. 20500

Dear President Clinton,

My name is Carol Andrews and I am just 33 years old. I may never live to see 35. I have cancer.

On November 4, 1993, my 33rd birthday, I woke up with terrible abdominal pains. On November 5, I went into surgery for what doctors believed would be an appendectomy.

I awakened four hours later with my doctor standing over me. Stage III colon cancer, he said. It had spread to the lymph nodes. A 50 percent chance of dying in the next five years. *Fifty percent.* My life had changed forever, irrevocably. Even if I survive, I will live the rest of my life fearing it will come back someday.

I'm young, and up until then I was healthy. I don't smoke, almost never drink, I eat well and have no family history of colon cancer. They have no explanation for this. I didn't bring this upon myself and I didn't deserve it. I'm a good, decent, hard-working person.

For almost a year now, I have undergone chemotherapy every week. I get sick, I feel tired all the time, yet I go to work eight hours a day, five days a week. I try so hard to lead a normal life.

But none of this is the most frustrating part of cancer. What frustrates and worries me most is this: As a cancer patient, even if I survive this and live another 50 years, my cancer always will be a pre-existing condition under current insurance guidelines. Sure, I can take a chance and get a new job somewhere, or move to a new place, and I'll be covered by insurance - except for cancer. So if the cancer reoccurs, I face financial ruin trying to pay for treatment.

Unless the law changes things, or I wish to risk losing all my family owns, I can never take a better job. I can never fulfill my dream of opening a bed & breakfast in the Rocky Mountains or New England. And unless my family chooses to leave me behind, my limitations become theirs. I'm trapped, they're trapped, and it's a horrible, horrible feeling.

As Congress considers the health reform issue, I appeal to you to keep me and my family, and the millions like us, in your thoughts. Please work to pass a health reform bill that will

COMPLETED

2-1-93

Dear Mrs Clinton
    I am happy to wish you & your family Congratulations on your election! We are all hoping for change.
    I am a 66 yr old retired RN disabled with Rheumatoid Arthritis & HBP.
    I have Medicare & BC/BS supplemental insurance which costs $64.50 a month. My SS check is $641.00 less the 64.50. My medications cost me

Citizens from all over the country wrote letters to the President and First Lady describing their difficulties in finding affordable health care for themselves and their families.

Putting People First

By 1992, people were working longer hours and spending less time with their children. Incomes kept going down, while the cost of health care, housing, and education kept going up. Millions of working parents were supporting their children on the one hand and their elderly parents on the other. More working Americans were falling into poverty, and social ills were on the rise. The welfare system had become a trap for America's poor and a symbol of government failure.

Since President Franklin D. Roosevelt's New Deal, Americans have embraced the idea that the federal government has basic obligations to ensure the health and security of its workers. Social Security has kept millions of elderly Americans from poverty; unemployment insurance has kept families afloat when a parent loses a job; Medicaid and Medicare have protected the poor and elderly in times of illness.

Bill Clinton argued that government could be a force for positive change in people's lives. As President, he committed his administration to reforming welfare and extending quality health care and retirement security to millions of Americans.

Top: President Clinton speaks to the Navajo Nation to discuss how access to technology can lead to economic opportunity.
Bottom: The First Lady visits Trinity College Community Child Center to highlight President Clinton's Childcare Initiative.

alth care to all, because we don't have a person to waste." —PRESIDENT CLINTON, 01/19/99

Building One America

In the late 20th century, the United States was growing more diverse as immigrants from every part of the world came seeking a chance at the American Dream. At the same time, for many of our citizens—some whose ancestors arrived on these shores in slave ships—the full promise of America remained out of reach. Social and economic gaps that divided our country were widening. Then, in 1992, riots ripped through Los Angeles. Americans of all backgrounds wondered whether our sense of community was being lost.

Bill Clinton took office determined to bring people together. In 1993, he created AmeriCorps, making it possible for Americans to earn money for college by "getting things done" in communities across the country. He also launched the first White House effort to promote racial reconciliation, and established a presidential office to pursue that goal. Through his policies, as well as through the power of the bully pulpit, the President sought to demonstrate that we, as Americans, could celebrate our differences while reaffirming our common humanity.

Top: South Central Los Angeles during 1992 riots.
Bottom: Presidential candidate Bill Clinton visits the area with U.S. Representative Maxine Waters.

"America is an idea. We're not one race. We're not one ethnic group. We're

BUILDING ONE AMERICA

Top to bottom: Town Hall meetings promoted dialogue on tolerance and inclusion; President Clinton kept this photo of Ricky Ray, a teenage hemophiliac with HIV, on his desk to inspire him to focus on AIDS; the President with members of a graduating class of AmeriCorps volunteers.

e religious group. We share a common piece of ground here." —PRESIDENT CLINTON, 07/04/95

"WE COME HERE TODAY TO SAY WE COULD NOT HAVE DONE IT IF BRAVE AMERICANS HAD NOT FIRST WALKED ACROSS THE EDMUND PETTUS BRIDGE.

YES, WE HAVE COME A MIGHTY LONG WAY. BUT OUR JOURNEY IS NOT OVER, FOR DESPITE OUR UNPRECEDENTED PROSPERITY AND REAL SOCIAL PROGRESS, THERE ARE STILL WIDE AND DISTURBING DISPARITIES THAT FALL ALONG THE COLOR LINE—IN HEALTH AND INCOME, IN EDUCATIONAL ACHIEVEMENT AND PERCEPTIONS OF JUSTICE.

MY FELLOW AMERICANS, THERE ARE STILL BRIDGES YET TO CROSS."

—PRESIDENT CLINTON, MARCH 5, 2000

The President, with Jesse Jackson, Coretta Scott King, Congressman John Lewis and other civil rights leaders, marches across the Edmund Pettus Bridge, Selma, Alabama.

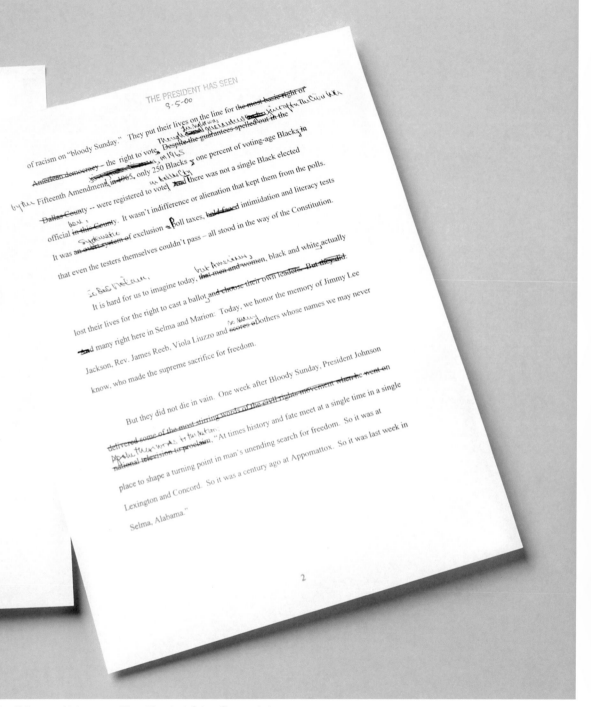

e President's handwritten changes on his speech mmemorating the 35th anniversary of the 1965 Voting ghts March, led by Martin Luther King, Jr., in Selma, Alabama. e march woke the nation to inequalities in America; six months later, President Johnson signed the Voting Rights Act into law. On March 5, 2000, President Clinton walked across the Edmund Pettus Bridge with many of the people who had risked their lives on "Bloody Sunday" in 1965. He later wrote, "I loved that day in Selma. Once again, I was swept back across the years to my boyhood longing for and belief in an America without a racial divide. Once again, I returned to the emotional core of my political life..."

Making
Communities Safer

In the 30 years before President Clinton took office, violent crime in America had more than tripled. As communities struggled, the federal government, bogged down in a partisan debate over the merits of punishment versus prevention, offered little support.

President Clinton sought to restore a sense of responsibility both to government and to the people who lived in troubled communities. He believed that by expanding the number of police, giving them the tools to do their jobs, and creating partnerships between communities and law enforcement, we could build a safer America. For eight years, the Clinton Administration pursued the two objectives of tougher punishment and smarter prevention—combining stiffer penalties and more police with innovative programs for youth and commonsense gun laws.

Results were dramatic. The crime rate fell every year that Bill Clinton was President, reaching a 27-year low by the time he left office. The murder rate dropped to its lowest point since 1966, and gun-related violence was reduced by nearly half.

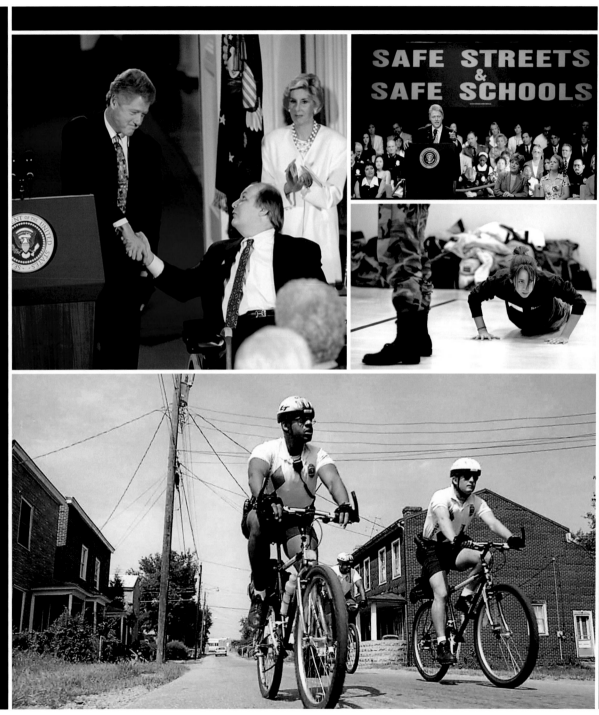

Clockwise from top left: President Clinton at the signing of the Brady Bill; delivering an address on juvenile crime at a high school in California; alternative "boot camps" deal with young offenders; bike patrol as part of new "neighborhood policy" initiated in high-crime areas.

"Modern science has confirmed what we first learned from ancient faiths: the most important fact

Science and Technology

In 1993, the information age was in its early stages. The Internet had only 50 sites, e-mail was used mainly by scientists, and few industries had begun to harness the power of information technology. President Clinton and Vice President Gore, however, recognized that a profound social and economic transformation was under way. They set out to accelerate innovation and, just as important, to ensure that all Americans would reap the benefits of the new era.

Although decades of U.S. government investment had made many of the technological innovations possible, by 1992 America's commitment was lagging behind its competitors'. The Clinton Administration put the United States back in the lead, making record investments in cutting-edge research and development.

Change on this scale brought new challenges as well as new opportunities. President Clinton worked to make sure that science, especially in the realms of genetics and biotechnology, would serve humanity without undermining our values, freedoms, and rights.

esident Clinton signs the Telecommunications Act, a sweeping orm of laws facilitating the information revolution.

Top to bottom: Announcing investments for technology in underserved communities; *Informatics meets Genomics,* one of a series of Millennium Evenings featuring Dr. Vinton Cerf and Dr. Eric Lander; a CD containing the entire human genome.

this earth is our common humanity." —PRESIDENT CLINTON, 06/26/00

Learning Across A Lifetime

American prosperity has long depended on the education of its citizens. Taking office at a time when vanishing jobs and economic competition from overseas were undermining the nation's spirit, Bill Clinton believed America could prosper again if more people could gain the skills to compete in the emerging information-based economy.

Over the next eight years, millions of Americans got a better chance of acquiring the education they needed to make the most of their lives. Academic standards were raised. Class sizes were reduced. Pre-school, after-school, and adult education programs were expanded. In addition, the nation saw the largest increase in college aid since the GI Bill sent a generation of veterans to school following World War II.

As a result, America's public school students, even those in disadvantaged communities, raised their test scores. A greater percentage than ever went on to college. More adults got the tools they needed to find good jobs. And America entered the 21st century the undisputed leader of the global economy.

Top: President Clinton with a student at an elementary school in Chicago.
Bottom: Educational opportunities for adults, together with training for new skills, expanded employment opportunities for a wide range of Americans.

Children's portraits of President Clinton.

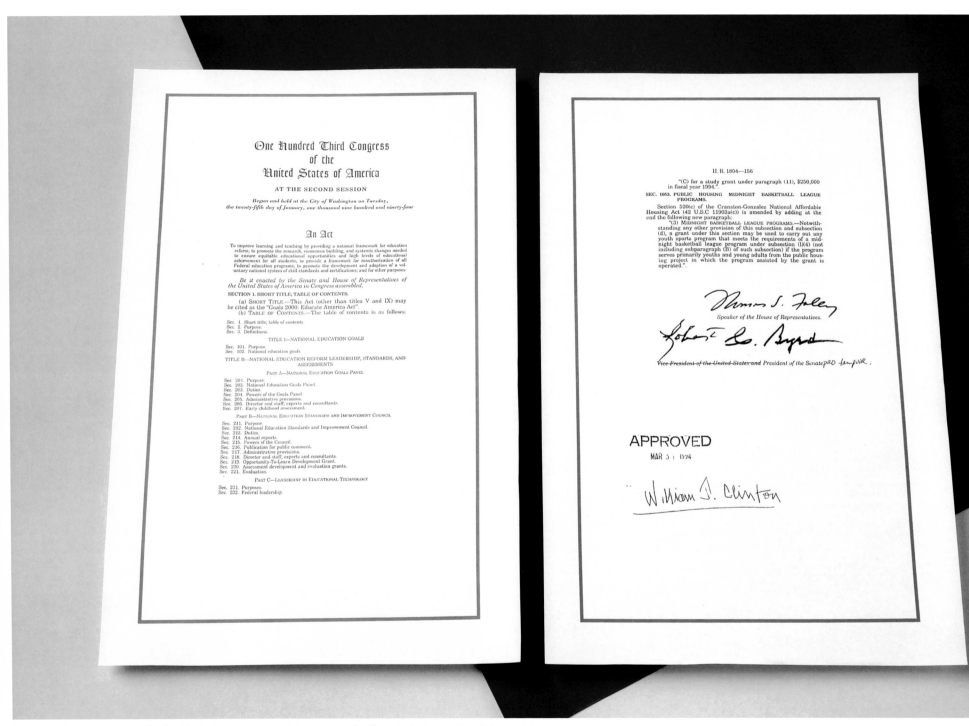

Goals 2000: Educate America Act. The President's vision for school reform was rooted in the belief that every child has the ability to meet high academic standards and no child should be excluded from a quality education. His Goals 2000 legislation required states to create educational standards describing what each student must learn at each stage, as well as tests to see if students were actually meeting these standards. In 1996, 16 states had measurable standards in place. By 2000, that number had grown to 49.

"EVERY 8-YEAR-OLD MUST BE
ABLE TO READ; EVERY 12-YEAR-OLD
MUST BE ABLE TO LOG ON TO THE
INTERNET; EVERY 18-YEAR-OLD
MUST BE ABLE TO GO TO COLLEGE;
AND EVERY ADULT AMERICAN MUST
BE ABLE TO KEEP ON LEARNING
FOR A LIFETIME."

—PRESIDENT CLINTON, 02/04/97

The Fight For Power

The 1990s were a decade of intense partisanship, with a growing ideological divide between Democrats and Republicans. From the start of the Clinton Presidency, the administration's opponents waged an unprecedented fight for power. Seeking to steer America sharply to the right, Republican leaders pursued a radical agenda through radical means.

They used new tools and tactics—lawsuits, investigations, new partisan media, front groups, a secret slush fund, and deeply divisive rhetoric—in their battle for political supremacy. The normal give-and-take of public life gave way to what many called the "politics of personal destruction."

After the Republicans won the Congress in 1994, the fight for power culminated in two government shutdowns and an impeachment battle, bringing partisan opposition to a new high and attempting to deny the very legitimacy of the President's election.

Throughout, the President and his administration continued to enjoy high public approval ratings and to implement much of their agenda. However, these battles took a heavy toll, affecting the lives, reputations, and financial well-being of many public servants and private citizens, and wasting millions of taxpayer dollars on investigations.

Top: Washington during the partial shutdown of the federal government, 1995. Bottom: Furloughed Social Security Administration workers gather in protest.

"I think one of the great problems in the Republican party is t

Top: Despite partisan politics, President Clinton stays focused on the nation's priorities and vetoes the Republicans' plan for balancing the budget. The plan called for drastic cuts in funding for Medicaid, Medicare, education, and the environment.
Bottom: Newspaper headlines announcing the President's acquittal.

don't encourage you to be nasty." —NEWT GINGRICH, 10/95

Ideological Battles

After the 1994 elections, newly elected Republican lawmakers, under the leadership of Newt Gingrich, brought an ideological agenda and an intense brand of partisanship to Capitol Hill, rejecting compromise and attacking the character of their opponents.

These efforts culminated in the "battle of the budget." In late 1995, as the price for a balanced budget, the Congressional leadership demanded tax cuts for upper-income Americans and massive cuts in funding for health care, education, and the environment. When the President vetoed their plans, the G.O.P. forced two government shutdowns.

Strong public support for the administration's centrist approach of balancing the budget and investing in our future finally brought Congress back to the bargaining table, leading to the restoration of many of the proposed cuts and paving the way to a balanced budget.

The Politics of Persecution

In 1978, Congress passed the Independent Counsel Statute in response to the investigation of the Watergate break-in during the Nixon administration. The new law created a mechanism for investigations of the executive branch by an outside, or independent, prosecutor. Over the next 20 years, however, even many advocates of the law came to see it as deeply flawed. Prosecutors had virtually unlimited discretion to investigate whatever they wanted. Inquiries stretched on for years—costing millions, destroying reputations, and achieving little good. The law became a potent political tool.

By 1998, seven separate investigations of the Clinton Administration were under way by Special Counsels. They cost well over $100 million in taxpayer dollars. The Starr investigation alone spent $70 million. None of these efforts yielded a conviction for public misconduct. In 1999, both parties in Congress allowed the Independent Counsel Statute to expire.

Excerpts from Senator Dale Bumpers' handwritten notes for the January 21, 1999, speech he gave on the Senate floor, in which he argued against impeachment.

Conclusion

I THE American people are now — & for some time have been asking to be allowed a good night's sleep for an end to this "national nightmare."

It is ~~up to you~~ a legitimate request. ~~their~~ Their voices deserve to be heard. I've said "cast a vote vs. polls – but I never said cast an irresponsible vote to show your courage."

It's Time To get back to their agenda.

HST Trust The People

A New Culture of Confrontation

In the partisan wars that had raged since the mid-1960s, neither side was completely blameless. But the rise of the "New Right" in the 1980s led to a dramatic increase in personal attacks by conservatives on their opponents. In 1995, when the Republican party took control of Congress, self-described Republican "revolutionaries" used their subpoena power to investigate opponents, as the rise of the 24-hour news cycle fueled the media's hunger for constant scandal, real or imagined, and the lines between tabloid and mainstream journalism became blurred. Rumors and accusations spread quickly on the Internet, gained currency on talk radio, and then appeared in television news reports and major newspapers—sometimes in the course of a single day.

In this combustible climate, the Congressional Republicans took the politics of personal destruction to a new level, using the subpoena power to investigate Democrats, attack them in a number of public hearings, and attempt to change popular public policies by discrediting the President and members of his administration personally.

The Impeachment Battle

In 1994, Kenneth Starr was appointed to investigate a failed real estate investment, known as Whitewater, that the Clintons had made in the 1970s. Finding no evidence of wrongdoing on the part of the Clintons, Starr repeatedly expanded the scope of his investigation. Witnesses complained that Starr and his staff would threaten them with jail in an attempt to get them to change their stories. In January 1998, Starr began to look into the President's testimony about his relationship with Monica Lewinsky, given in a deposition in a civil suit. The suit was later dismissed as having no legal or factual merit.

In September 1998, President Clinton acknowledged that he had not been forthcoming about the relationship. On this basis, Starr, the Republican Congressional leadership, and their allies launched an impeachment drive that the overwhelming majority of constitutional scholars said was unjustified. The impeachment battle was not about the Constitution or rule of law, but was instead a quest for power that the President's opponents could not win at the ballot box. The constitutional crisis ended with the President's acquittal in the Senate.

PROTECTING THE EARTH

"AS WE BEGIN THE NEW MILLENNIUM, LET OUR GIFT TO THE FUTURE BE A NEW EFFORT, TOGETHER ACROSS PARTY LINES, TO CLEAN OUR AIR, TO ENSURE SAFE WATER, AND TO PRESERVE HEALTHY, THRIVING LANDS."

"Now is the time to join our citizens and our governments, our businesses and our industries, in the fight agai

Protecting The Earth

At the dawn of the 20th century, President Theodore Roosevelt challenged the nation to take "the long look ahead" and ensure that one generation's progress does not come at the expense of future generations. Almost a century later, President Clinton and Vice President Gore took up this challenge, rededicating the nation to protecting precious natural treasures at home while restoring America's environmental leadership abroad.

Despite pitched battles with entrenched interests focused on self-serving short-term gains, the Clinton Administration protected more land than any other administration in history. It enacted the strongest protections ever for the air we breathe, improved the quality of drinking water for millions of citizens, and led the world to confront new environmental challenges that require cooperation across borders and ideological divides. These environmental successes, coming in an era of unprecedented economic growth, proved that a strong economy and a healthy environment can go hand in hand.

Top right: Grand Staircase-Escalante National Monument, and bottom left, California's ocean cliffs, part of the more than eight million acres protected during the Clinton Administration. Top left: The Vice President and Prime Minister Ryutaro Hashimoto of Japan at the Convention on Climate Change, Kyoto. Center: The President speaks at the Grand Canyon. Bottom right: At the signing of the Safe Drinking Water Act.

Top: Under President Clinton, the U.S. military became a more rapidly deployable, flexible armed force—powered with the most advanced weapons and communications systems. Bottom: Fragment from a decommissioned Soviet nuclear submarine.

"As we reduce the global stockpiles of weapons of mass destruction, we must also reduce t

Preparing for New Threats

The threat from the Soviet Union had driven U.S. national security and military strategy for nearly 50 years when the Communist government collapsed in 1991, leaving America as the world's sole superpower. Old threats were now diminished, but did not disappear. Thousands of Soviet nuclear, biological, and chemical weapons still existed, and new, more diffuse dangers emerged: the spread of weapons of mass destruction and the rise of global terrorism.

NATO remained an indispensable alliance, and under President Clinton's leadership it expanded with the admission of three former Soviet satellites—Poland, Hungary, and the Czech Republic. But a wider range of allies were needed to ensure America's security in the 21st century. President Clinton thus made it a priority to both build new partnerships with old adversaries and strengthen relations with longtime allies. At home, he dramatically increased funding for counter-terrorism, reversed a decade of decline in defense spending, and equipped the U.S. military with the advanced technology it would need to respond rapidly and decisively to coming threats.

Top: President Clinton places flowers at the Oklahoma City Memorial.
Bottom: with U.S. troops in Bosnia

"You have to help your children remember their history, but you must not force them to relive the

Confronting Conflict, Making Peace

In 1992, the Cold War between the United States and the Soviet Union was over, but deadly conflicts still raged in many parts of the world. Some, like the war in the Balkans and the Israeli–Palestinian dispute, threatened the stability of regions vital to America and its allies. Many involved ethnic and religious disputes that, if exploited by ruthless leaders, could throw large parts of the planet into turmoil. All tested whether America, the world's only remaining superpower, would use its power for the common good.

President Clinton believed strongly that the United States should mobilize its strength in the cause of peace. He used diplomacy where possible, military force where necessary, to resolve conflicts. He traveled to every part of the world urging aggrieved peoples to choose reconciliation over revenge. Often, these efforts achieved breakthroughs that ended wars and saved lives. In some cases, bitter quarrels still defied resolution. Yet in every case, President Clinton's willingness to go the extra mile for peace ensured that American power would be respected, not resented, in the new global age.

Clockwise from top left: The President with his foreign policy team; hopes for the future in Northern Ireland; children in Kosovo; historic handshake between Yitzhak Rabin and Yasser Arafat; with King Hussein of Jordan.

ey deserve to live in their tomorrows, not in your yesterdays." —PRESIDENT CLINTON, 08/28/00

"YOUR PRIME MINISTER WAS A MARTYR FOR PEACE, BUT HE WAS A VICTIM OF HATE. SURELY WE MUST LEARN FROM HIS MARTYRDOM THAT IF PEOPLE CANNOT LET GO OF THE HATRED OF THEIR ENEMIES, THEY RISK SOWING THE SEEDS OF HATRED AMONG THEMSELVES. I ASK YOU, THE PEOPLE OF ISRAEL, ON BEHALF OF MY NATION THAT KNOWS ITS OWN LONG LITANY OF LOSS, FROM ABRAHAM LINCOLN TO PRESIDENT KENNEDY TO MARTIN LUTHER KING, DO NOT LET THAT HAPPEN TO YOU."

—PRESIDENT CLINTON, 11/06/95

President Clinton and Israeli Prime Minister Yitzhak Rabin talk in the Oval Office, 1993. In November of 1995 Prime Minister Rabin addressed a peace rally in Tel Aviv, saying, "I have been a military man for 27 years. I fought as long as there was no chance for peace. I believe there is such a chance now..." As he was leaving the rally, Rabin was shot by an extremist who wanted to kill the peace process.

mulka and stone, President Clinton's personal
ementos from the funeral of Prime Minister Rabin.

The President and First Lady attend the funeral of
Israeli Prime Minister Yitzhak Rabin. President Clinton
later wrote, "We had become friends in that unique
way that people do when they are in a struggle
that they believe is unique and good. With every
encounter, I came to respect and care for him more.
By the time he was killed, I had come to love him
as I had rarely loved another man."

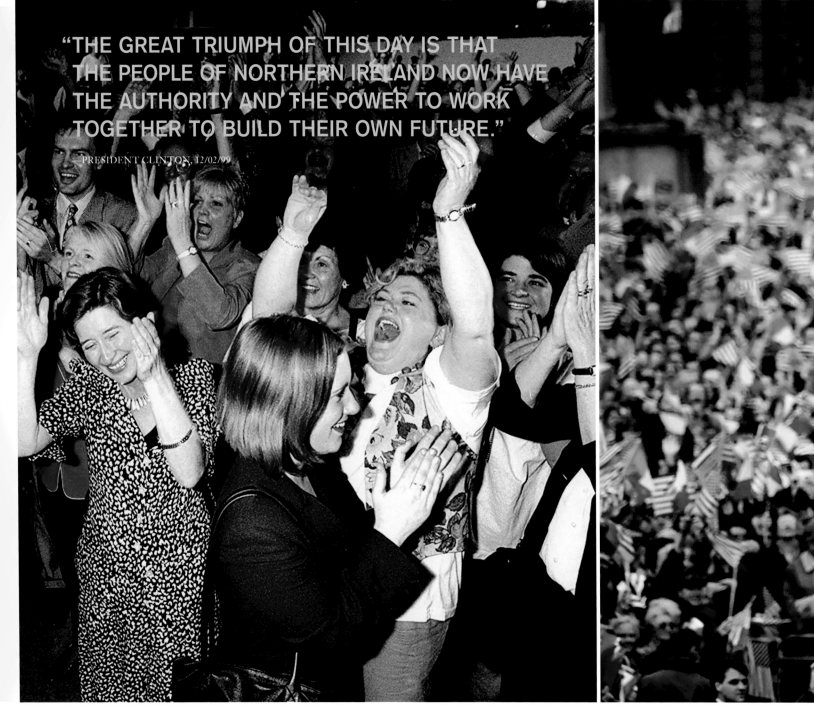

"THE GREAT TRIUMPH OF THIS DAY IS THAT THE PEOPLE OF NORTHERN IRELAND NOW HAVE THE AUTHORITY AND THE POWER TO WORK TOGETHER TO BUILD THEIR OWN FUTURE."
—PRESIDENT CLINTON, 12/02/99

People celebrate in Belfast after the announcement of the approval of the Northern Ireland peace agreement on May 23, 1998.

1995, President Clinton was the first American president to vel to Northern Ireland; his direct appeals to the Irish people vanized support for peace. He traveled to Belfast for the t time as President in December 2000 to speed progress

towards disarmament and other key provisions of the Good Friday Accords. Though implementation proved difficult, the agreement advanced peace and prosperity in the ancestral homeland of millions of Americans.

The Northern Ireland Political Chess Piece Process was a gift to President Clinton during his trip to Belfast in 1998. The sculpture's caricature pieces depict figures on both sides of the negotiating process.

Building a Global Community

By the fall of 1992, celebration of the Cold War's end gave way to grave uncertainty about what was coming next for America in the world. America was lagging competitively. U.S. alliances and institutions that had served America so well during the Cold War appeared outdated. There were fears that Russia was headed toward a Communist backlash; that the nuclear neighbors India and Pakistan would go to war; that the newly liberated countries of eastern Europe would become a gray zone of insecurity.

At home, political leaders called for America to pull away from the world and withdraw troops from western Europe and Korea. The Clinton Administration, however, believed that an increasingly globalized world required American leadership. President Clinton sought to redefine Cold War-era alliances and reorient them to new challenges; build new relationships with old adversaries; and recognize the importance of new emerging economies.

Eight years later, America's alliances stood strong, and the United States entered the 21st century as the world's leading force for peace and prosperity.

In partnership with democratic allies, President Clinton reshaped old institutions and initiated new ones.

"I hope that in the years ahead... America chooses to be a part of the world; to share the risks and opportunit

Top to bottom: Presidents Yeltsin and Clinton at a press conference; nesting dolls of world leaders (gift of Boris Yeltsin); welcoming Prime Minister Tony Blair in Washington.

...AND TO
IS A GLOBA
WITH US, F
—PRESIDENT CLINTON, 12

"I HOPE THAT IN THE YEARS AHEAD...AMERICA CHOOSES TO BE A PART OF THE WORLD, WITH A CLEAR HEAD AND A STRONG HEART; TO SHARE THE RISKS AND OPPORTUNITIES..."

Building a Global Community

By the fall of 1992, celebration of the Cold War's end gave way to grave uncertainty about what was coming next for America in the world. America was lagging competitively. U.S. alliances and institutions that had served America so well during the Cold War appeared outdated. There were fears that Russia was headed toward a Communist backlash; that the nuclear neighbors India and Pakistan would go to war; that the newly liberated countries of eastern Europe would become a gray zone of insecurity.

At home, political leaders called for America to pull away from the world and withdraw troops from western Europe and Korea. The Clinton administration, however, believed that an increasingly globalized world required American leadership. President Clinton sought to redefine Cold War–era alliances and reorient them to new challenges; build new relationships with old adversaries; and recognize the importance of new emerging economies.

Eight years later, America's alliances stood strong, and the United States entered the 21st century as the world's leading force for peace and prosperity.

Russia

China

Korea

til ultimately there is a global community of free nations, working with us, for peace and security." —PRESIDENT CLINTON, 12/08/00

Kente cloth (gift of Jerry John Rawlings, President of the Republic of Ghana) and a contemporary mask of President Clinton's face from Kenya.

President Rawlings of Ghana drapes kente cloth on President Clinton during the arrival ceremony, where he was greeted by hundreds of thousands of well-wishers. The historic trip to Africa was the most extensive to that continent of any American president. A main goal was to establish a new partnership between America and Africa, which was experiencing vast changes as democracy spread and economic reforms gained strength.

Top to bottom: At the Grand Mosque in Dakar, Senegal; At the Nigerian National Assembly; the President and First Lady in Uganda; speech to South African parliament.

IN YOU, SIR, WE SEE PROOF THAT THE HUMAN SPIRIT CAN NEVER BE CRUSHED. FOR 27 YEARS, WE WATCHED YOU FROM YOUR PRISON CELL INSPIRE MILLIONS OF YOUR PEOPLE WITH YOUR SPIRIT AND YOUR WORDS. AND WHEN YOU EMERGED, INSTEAD OF RETRIBUTION FOR PAST WRONG, YOU SOUGHT PEACE AND FREEDOM AND EQUALITY FOR YOUR PEOPLE."

—PRESIDENT CLINTON, 10/17/94

President Clinton visits Robben Island prison with Nelson Mandela. After Mandela was elected the first black president of South Africa, the two men quickly established a warm and close personal relationship. President Clinton often calls his friend Madiba, an affectionate tribal term for elder statesman.

Top to bottom: The President and First Lady lay brick in Capetown, South Africa; with Senegalese president Abdou Diouf at the "Door of No Return" at the former slave-trading outpost on Goree Island; with President Nelson Mandela.

Expanding Our Shared Prosperity

Globalization was the defining reality of the Clinton Presidency. In the span of several years, new technologies transformed the ways that people worked, learned, and lived. A revolution in travel, commerce, and communications meant that by the late 1990s more people and goods moved from continent to continent in a single hour than in the entire 19th century.

Globalization rewarded countries whose businesses, workers, and capital could move quickly to support promising ventures. The Clinton Administration seized this opportunity, opening new markets for U.S. products and helping to create millions of jobs for Americans. As the new century approached, however, the gap between rich and poor nations became a matter of growing concern. President Clinton's view was that globalization could benefit the poorest countries—but only if the United States led a worldwide effort to "put a human face on the global economy." To turn this vision into reality, the administration took historic steps toward reducing poverty, debt, and disease in the developing world, giving poorer nations a better chance to prosper.

Signing five of nearly 300 trade agreements, top to bottom: Permanent Normal Trade Relations with China; NAFTA; Summit of the Americas; GATT; African Growth and Opportunity Act.

"Every penny we spend on reducing worldwide poverty, improving literacy, wiping out disea

Clockwise from top left: Administration efforts helped resolve the 1998 Asian financial crisis; the Africa Growth and Opportunity Act created jobs in South Africa; the First Lady at the Women's Empowerment Center in the Gaza Strip; results of increased funding for vaccine programs in India; the President with musician Bono after meeting on international debt relief for poor countries.

l come back to us and our children a hundredfold." —PRESIDENT CLINTON, 12/14/00

Top to bottom: The First Lady at a victory celebration as U.S. senator-elect for the State of New York; reading to children; delivering the keynote address at the U.N. Conference on Women, Beijing, China.

"It is time for us to say... and the world to hear, that it is no longer acceptabl

The Work of The First Lady

Hillary Clinton was one of our country's most active First Ladies, fulfilling the traditional duties of the office, while assuming an unprecedented role in policy making at home and diplomacy abroad. Mrs. Clinton was the first professional woman to serve as First Lady, the first to have an office in the West Wing, and the first to launch her own campaign for an elective post, which she won, joining the U.S. Senate in 2001.

Hillary Clinton was a leading voice for children and working families. After his election, President Clinton asked his wife to continue championing these issues. As First Lady, Mrs. Clinton helped shape policies to improve health care, education, child care, and foster care. With the President, she hosted two conferences on child care which played a key role in developing the President's Child Care Initiative. She worked to reform our nation's foster care system and to promote adoption, resulting in the passage of the Adoption and Safe Family Act of 1997. She also traveled extensively, becoming one of the world's most powerful voices for women's rights, human rights, and democracy. A strong supporter of arts and culture, the First Lady fought to save historic monuments, sites, and artifacts, and made the Clinton White House a showcase for American creativity.

Statue with embedded shrapnel, given during the First Lady's trip to Bosnia, 1995. She kept the statue in her office in the White House as a reminder, she said, "of the great price so many women have paid to bring justice and peace to all of us."

discuss women's rights as separate from human rights." —HILLARY RODHAM CLINTON, 09/05/95

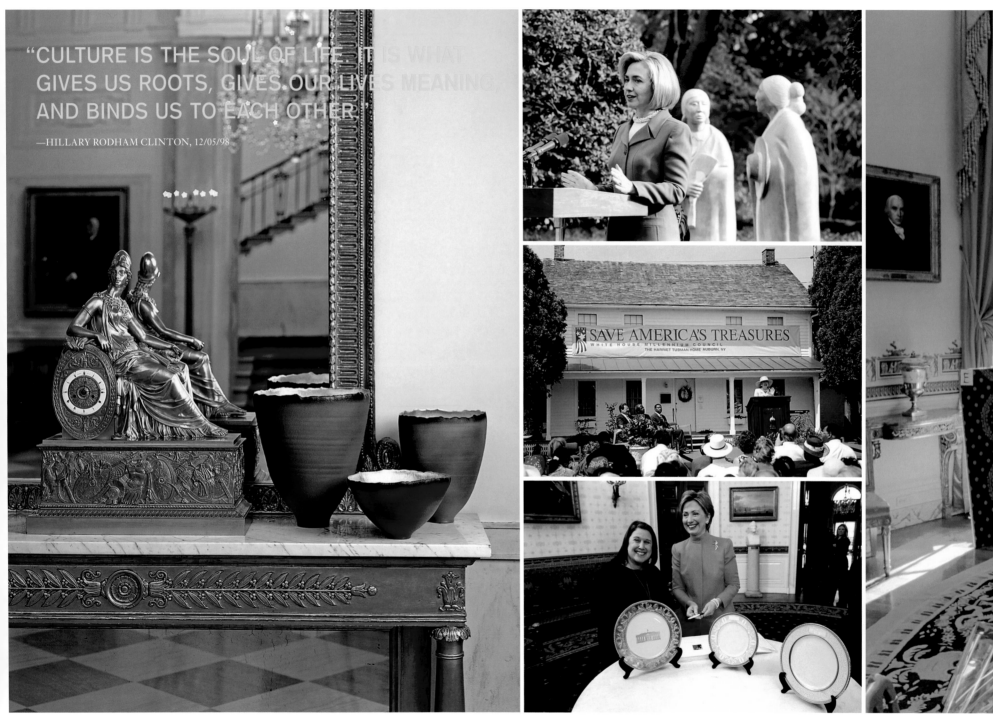

"CULTURE IS THE SOUL OF LIFE. IT IS WHAT
GIVES US ROOTS, GIVES OUR LIVES MEANING,
AND BINDS US TO EACH OTHER."

—HILLARY RODHAM CLINTON, 12/05/98

The First Lady made the White House a showcase for fine examples of American crafts. Above: *Prayer Bowls* by Cheryl C. Williams, in the Entrance Hall; Far right: *Yellow Pair* by Dante Marioni, 1993, photographed in the Yellow Oval Room of the White House.

Top to bottom: In the Jacqueline Kennedy garden presenting sculptures by Native American artists; at a Save America's Treasures event in Auburn, New York; the First Lady was actively involved in the project to design new china to commemorate the 200th Anniversary of the White House.

The First Lady was actively involved in every detail of the 5-year renovation of the Blue Room. She also led a series of Save America's Treasures tours to historic sites to increase awareness and raise funds in support of restoration projects and the preservation of America's heritage of monuments, documents, and art treasures. Mrs. Clinton's love of sculpture spurred her to promote the creation of the White House National Sculpture Garden, which millions of visitors enjoy.

The President and First Lady at the 1997 inaugural ball.

THE CLINTONS
EARLY YEARS TO WHITE HOUSE YEARS

The Mezzanine of the Main Gallery is largely devoted to Bill Clinton's life from his early boyhood in Arkansas to the Clinton family's years in the White House. His passion for music, his early interest in politics and public service, his love of westerns, the dreams that drove him, and the way that the Clintons made the White House into a true family home are captured in this section of the Museum. Exhibits offer a warm and personal look at the events, artifacts, and memories of the 42nd President of the United States, including collections from White House holiday celebrations, china settings from official state events, and gifts to the President from people all over the world.

Among the highlights of the mezzanine exhibits are gifts of State,
a table setting for a White House dinner, and a satin ball gown
(designed by Vera Wang) worn by the First Lady at the state dinner
for Chinese President Jiang Zemin.

Arkansas in 1946 was a place rooted in tradition, yet poised on the cusp of sweeping change.

Tens of thousands of veterans were streaming home from World War II, eager to start new lives and new families. Among them was William Jefferson Blythe, a native Texan who had served in the army as a mechanic and was now beginning work as a salesman. After a whirlwind courtship, he married a small-town girl from southwest Arkansas, Virginia Cassidy. Before their son was born, Blythe died in a tragic car accident, trying to make it to Hope on a long trip from Chicago, where he worked and where they planned to live after their baby was born. With a resolute faith in her destiny, and the sturdy support of friends and relatives, Virginia pressed ahead with her life, determined to be a good mother to William Jefferson Blythe III, born in Hope, Arkansas, on August 19, 1946. There were immense challenges ahead for her and for Arkansas—but nothing that couldn't be conquered with a firm faith in the future.

The Early Years

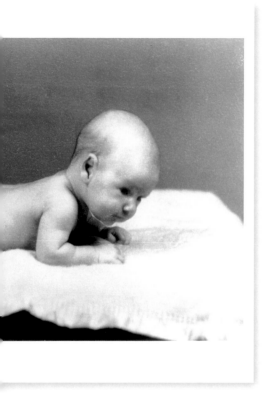

ckwise from left: At a birthday party in Hope, Arkansas, 1950; Hope, Arkansas, 1952; with his mother Virginia, 1963; Billy Blythe (far left)
oy picture of William Jefferson Blythe III, born August 19, 1946; Virginia at Miss Mary's Kindergarten, Hope, Arkansas; grandfather Eldridge Cassidy
d William Jefferson Blythe, Bill Clinton's parents; with Roger Clinton, in his grocery store, Hope, Arkansas, c. 1940.

America changed considerably over the years when Bill Clinton attended school.

In the autumn of 1960, Dwight Eisenhower presided over a comfortably conformist nation, still dominated by memories of the war. Four years later, the New Frontier had come and gone, and Lyndon Johnson was taking his first strides toward tackling civil rights and the war on poverty. Bill Clinton changed during those years as well. From the moment he was old enough to go to school, he loved the world of learning and the limitless possibilities it signaled. At Hot Springs High School, he was fortunate to come under the influence of several gifted teachers, including principal Johnnie Mae Mackey, and band instructor Virgil Spurlin. Music became a lifelong passion for the young saxophonist, who ultimately earned all-state honors. Perhaps more importantly, music taught him the rudiments of political organization, as he helped Mr. Spurlin plan the statewide competitions that brought hundreds of aspiring band performers to Hot Springs each year. Political conventions were quiet in comparison.

The Learning Years

Clockwise from left: Bill Clinton with the Hot Springs High School Band; 16-year-old high school student Bill Clinton shakes hands with President John F. Kennedy in the White House Rose Garden, 1963; Bill Clinton and Hillary Rodham at Yale Law School, 1972.

Bill Clinton never wavered in his determination to return home to Arkansas.

After finishing law school in 1973, he started teaching as a professor at the University of Arkansas Law School. He fell in love with Fayetteville and the hill country of North Arkansas, and soon was thinking about running for Congress against John Paul Hammerschmidt, a popular Republican incumbent. At first, it seemed hopeless: two years earlier, Hammerschmidt had coasted with 77 percent of the vote. But Watergate had dimmed the luster of Richard Nixon and his defenders, and Clinton ran a brilliant campaign in the rural hollows of the Ozarks, determined to meet as many voters as possible. It nearly worked. On Election Day in November 1974, he won 13 of 21 counties, but he lost the popular vote by a narrow margin of six thousand votes. The day after his defeat, he was out on the hustings again, thanking the voters for the experience of a lifetime.

...ckwise from top left: Virginia Clinton and others in Hot Springs campaigning for ...Clinton's bid for Congress, 1974; Governor Bill Clinton's inauguration, January 1987; ...nton is sworn in as the youngest governor in the United States in four decades, ...nuary 1979; Bill and Hillary on Election Eve, 1982.

Arkansas Campaigns

Hillary Rodham Clinton's life began at a time and place unique in history.

America in the mid-20th century was flush with prosperity and opportunities, and Hillary grew up with choices unavailable to girls and women of earlier generations. Coming of age on the crest of tumultuous social change, she immersed herself in the nation's political debates over the meaning of America and its role in the world. A wife, mother, lawyer, advocate, and First Lady, she became one of the world's most visible and influential voices on behalf of children, women, human rights and democracy. Although her parents and grandparents had never had her opportunities, they bestowed on her the promise of her nation and gave her the values and hopes that made her life and her contributions possible.

Hillary Rodham Clinton

Clockwise from left: Hillary Diane Rodham in 1958; with her paternal grandparents, Hannah and Hugh Rodham, in Scranton, Pennsylvania, 1948; Hillary's parents, Dorothy and Hugh Rodham, in Chicago, 1942, the year they married.

Clockwise from top left: Hillary and Bill during a volleyball game in Fayetteville, Arkansas, 1974; as an intern for the House Republican Conference, 1968; family picture with Chelsea in the living room of the governor's mansion, 1985; on their wedding day, October 11, 1975; at Maine South High, 1965.

Making This House a Home

When the Clintons arrived in Washington, Chelsea was 12 years old.

She had just left the only home she had ever known—the Governor's Mansion in Little Rock—and her parents were determined to make the White House a place the whole family could call home. They filled its rooms with the books, music, family photos, and other personal treasures from their lives together.

The Clintons converted the butler's pantry into a family kitchen, which became a favorite gathering spot. It was not uncommon to find the First Family enjoying dinner together, Chelsea and her friends raiding the refrigerator, the President watching a football game with the butlers, or Buddy and Socks looking for a leftover. Upstairs, you might find the Clintons gathered in the West Sitting Hall, unwinding after an event; or the family and friends watching television in the Solarium, or otherwise making themselves at home with history.

Clockwise from top left: view of the exhibit displaying personal photos of the Clinton family along with portraits and memorabilia given to them by people from all across the U.S.; the President and First Lady in the Oval Office; Chelsea dances with her father during a 50s-themed birthday party for the First Lady; Buddy plays with a tennis ball on a snowy White House lawn.

For his 49th birthday, White House staff threw President Clinton a surprise party with a Western theme.

Top to bottom: Virginia Kelley with her two sons at her last Christmas, 1993; dancing at Mrs. Clinton's themed birthday party, 1995; Chelsea relaxes with her father in the White House residence.

Top to bottom: The Clintons exchange Christmas presents with Tipper and Al Gore, 1997; Buddy and Socks go eye-to-eye; at Chelsea's high school graduation, 1997.

any heads of state as well as ordinary citizens sent saxophones
President Clinton as gifts. Left: Saxophone, made by Amati Krastice,
t of His Excellency Vaclav Havel, President of the Czech Republic.
ght: Tenor sax, made by Leblanc/Yanagisawa.

"Hillary made a music room for me in a little room on the top floor of the White House that we weren't using, that was way at the end of a hall, and it had two doors, so no one could hear me when I was playing. And I just go in there and I play—and no matter what else is going on, I can... play for 15 or 20 minutes and I'm full of energy and ready to start again."

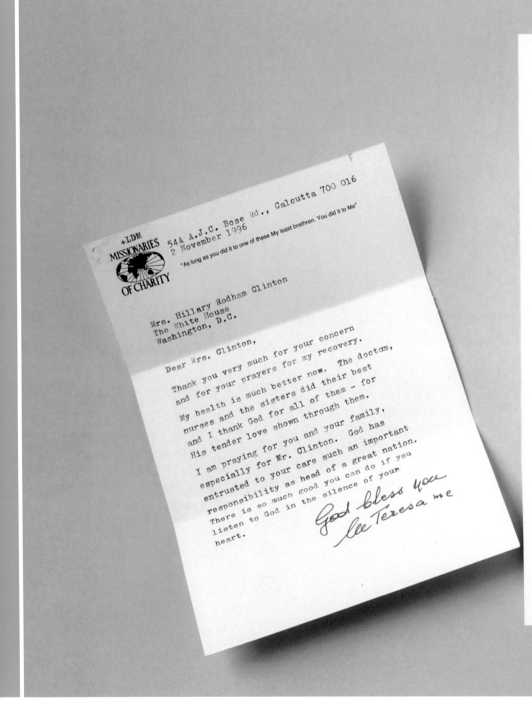

+LDM
MISSIONARIES OF CHARITY

54A A.J.C. Bose Rd., Calcutta 700 016
2 November 1996

"As long as you did it to one of these My least brethren. You did it to Me"

Mrs. Hillary Rodham Clinton
The White House
Washington, D.C.

Dear Mrs. Clinton,

Thank you very much for your concern and for your prayers for my recovery. My health is much better now. The doctors, nurses and the sisters did their best and I thank God for all of them - for His tender love shown through them.

I am praying for you and your family, especially for Mr. Clinton. God has entrusted to your care such an important responsibility as head of a great nation. There is so much good you can do if you listen to God in the silence of your heart.

God bless you
M Teresa me

Mr. President, Elvis, Bill from Little Rock, most important man in free world etc.,

It was an extraordinary week in the history of a small but noisy island of Ireland. Ali and I had the good fortune to be in Belfast on the first GOOD Friday they've had in 30 years... thank you for your part in that... and
... congratulations on your African tour, we had one ourselves. Last month U2 played 'John The Baptist' for you in Capetown and Johannesburg - but it was Elvis they were waiting for... Desmond Tutu, or 'The Arch' as he is known by his team, taught us this great word "UBUNTO" when we went to visit him - which he said was the essence of Africanism "I am because we are" was his explanation of it... something to do with empathy, interdependence, the interconnectedness of things...
this is what we like about your presidency, an outward looking White House, but you have no sea view, do you?

If your visit to the North, ends up in the South I should like to invite Hillary and yourself and Chelsea if she's coming, to stay. The 'Folly' is a beach house on the property and has been a hideaway for poets, musicians, hooligans and writers for a while now, is secure enough for Salman Rushdie and a lot more romantic than staying in the Park which I presume is the most practical - anyway, it's there - don't hesitate to ask for anything....

Regards,

Bono.

The President and First Lady received countless letters expressing concerns or gratitude from well-known people and ordinary citizens alike. Shown here are a note to Mrs. Clinton from Mother Theresa in thanks for her concern about her health, an invitation to the First Family from the musician Bono, and correspondence between the President and actor Paul Newman.

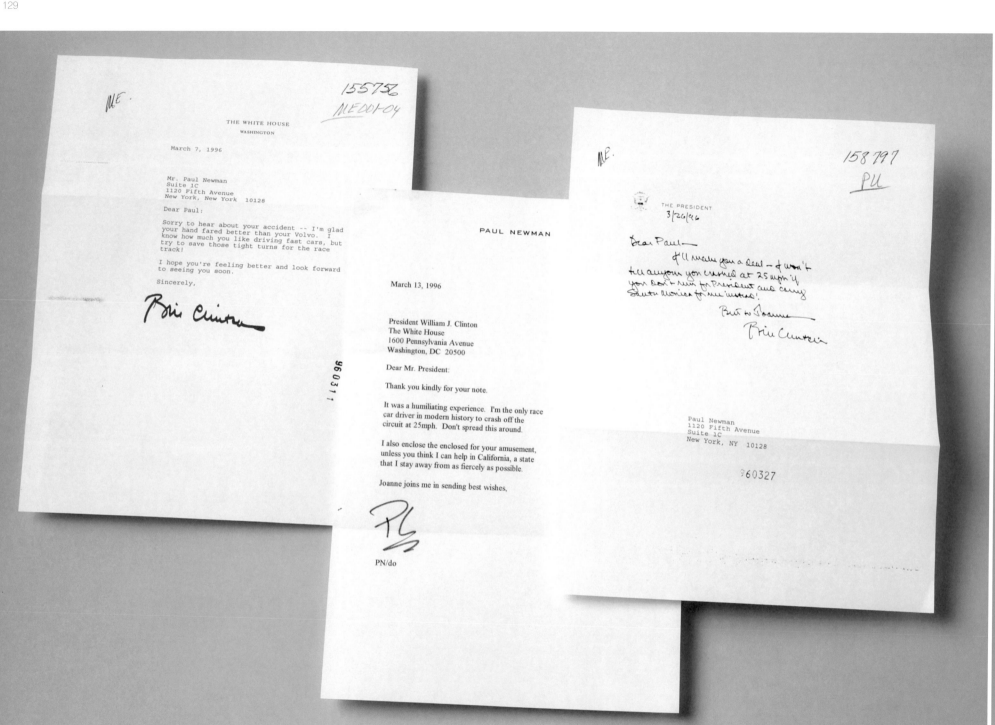

ME. 155756
ME001-04

THE WHITE HOUSE
WASHINGTON

March 7, 1996

Mr. Paul Newman
Suite 1C
1120 Fifth Avenue
New York, New York 10128

Dear Paul:

Sorry to hear about your accident -- I'm glad your hand fared better than your Volvo. I know how much you like driving fast cars, but try to save those tight turns for the race track!

I hope you're feeling better and look forward to seeing you soon.

Sincerely,

Bill Clinton

960311

PAUL NEWMAN

March 13, 1996

President William J. Clinton
The White House
1600 Pennsylvania Avenue
Washington, DC 20500

Dear Mr. President:

Thank you kindly for your note.

It was a humiliating experience. I'm the only race car driver in modern history to crash off the circuit at 25mph. Don't spread this around.

I also enclose the enclosed for your amusement, unless you think I can help in California, a state that I stay away from as fiercely as possible.

Joanne joins me in sending best wishes,

PN

PN/do

ME. 158797
PU

THE PRESIDENT
3/26/96

Dear Paul—
I'll make you a deal — I won't tell anyone you crashed at 25 mph if you don't run for President and carry South America for me instead!

Best to Joanne
Bill Clinton

Paul Newman
1120 Fifth Avenue
Suite 1C
New York, NY 10128

960327

On the first day the Clintons lived in the White House, they invited more than 3,000 Americans, and shook hands with every single one.

They were determined to invite more people than ever before to experience the history and beauty of the White House and the best of American culture. Over the next eight years, millions of Americans came to the White House—to enjoy picnics on the South Lawn, watch the arrivals of visiting heads of state, tour the White House, or attend thousands of other events that celebrated our nation's diversity. The Clintons expanded the Easter Egg Roll so that more children could take part, and they created a St. Patrick's Day celebration to bring people together for peace. One year, they turned the Congressional and press picnics into old-fashioned carnivals. And every year, thousands came to see the huge Christmas tree or to celebrate Chanukah, Ramadan, and Kwanza.

Clockwise from top left: Christmas, 2000; the annual Easter egg roll on the White House lawn; the First Lady admires a gingerbread house created by White House pastry chef Roland Mesnier.

Celebrations at The White House

Top: Children light a menorah in the Oval Office during Chanukah celebrations. Bottom: The President welcomes a young boy to the White House for a Ramadan celebration.

Clockwise from top left: view of the exhibit; a sample of the many gifts the President received; President Clinton receives a signed baseball bat from Cal Ripken.

People's Gifts

Americans love to give gifts to their Presidents and First Families.

It is a tradition of long standing, dating back at least to 1801, when grateful citizens presented a mammoth 1,235-pound cheese to Thomas Jefferson. By the 20th century, the gift-giving tradition had grown in popularity, with tens of thousands of gifts streaming to the White House every year. The gifts are as diverse as the nation. From the ordinary to the unique, they represent a vital connection between "We the people" and our Chief Executive, and directly express how we think he is doing.

The Clintons received tens of thousands of gifts from their fellow Americans. They commemorate important milestones or express affection, gratitude, and encouragement. Many reflect the President's interests in golf and music, or relate to Arkansas. Some are patriotic items such as flags and eagles. And, of course, there are many portraits of the First Family and of Buddy and Socks.

A painting given to the President titled "Elvis Introduces a Bill to Congress."

State Events

Every visit by a head of state involves elaborate protocol and ceremony. Clockwise from top left: view of the exhibit with formal table setting for a state dinner; at the arrival ceremony on the South Lawn for Jiang Zemin, President of the People's Republic of China, a 21-gun salute is fired; the Old Guard Fife and Drum Corps parade by the reviewing stand.

Welcoming world leaders to the White House has strategic as well as symbolic importance.

During the Clinton years, every element of these state events, from welcome to farewell, was designed to strengthen the bonds of friendship with the visiting leader and highlight our two countries' aspirations for the future.

The President and First Lady hosted representatives from emerging democracies such as South Africa and Ghana; traditional allies such as Britain and France; former foes such as Russia and China; neighbors such as Argentina, Mexico, Brazil, and Canada; and partners for peace such as Israel and Jordan.

State dinners are also opportunities to introduce world leaders to American culture and its diversity. During the Clinton years, the guest lists included men and women from all backgrounds and walks of life. Menus often represented a fusion of American and international cuisine. And entertainers ranged from Yo-Yo Ma to Stevie Wonder.

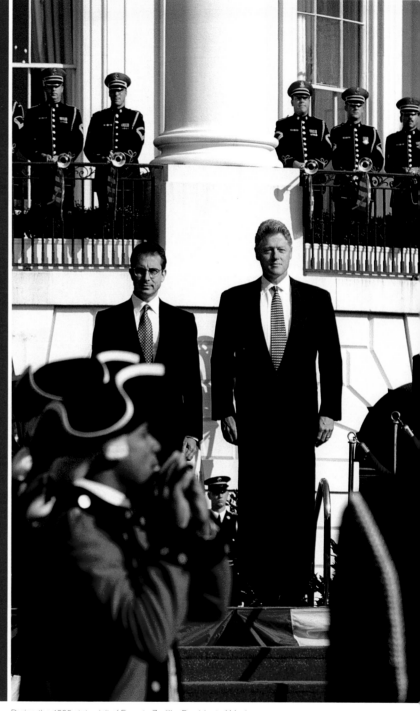

During the 1995 state visit of Ernesto Zedillo, President of Mexico, the Marine Band plays the national anthems of the visiting leader's country and the United States.

Clockwise from top left: A member of the Marine band plays the violin at a state dinner; state dinner for President and Mrs. Kim of South Korea, 1995; the President receives a gift from Premier Zhu Rongji of China and his wife, 1999; the First Lady dances with Václav Havel, President of the Czech Republic; dessert is brought out; state dinner for President and Mme. Jacques Chirac of France, 1996.

Gifts were often exchanged as gestures of diplomacy and goodwill. Left to right: *Coliseum in Rome*, stone mosaic, gift of His Holiness John Paul II; cloisonné plate, gift of His Excellency Jiang Zemin, President of the People's Republic of China; bronze ballerina, gift of The Honorable Anatoly Sobchak, Mayor of Saint Petersburg, Russian Federation.

The Clinton Oval Office

The Oval Office is the epicenter of the American presidency.

The modern-day Oval Office was created in 1909, when President William Howard Taft expanded the West Wing. In 1934, President Franklin D. Roosevelt had the room moved to its current location in the southwest corner of the West Wing.

Since then, every President has regarded the Oval Office as both a ceremonial room and a working office. President Clinton used the Oval Office as a place to conduct the daily business of the nation, sign legislation, meet with foreign heads of state, and deliver important addresses to the American people. While he also maintained a working office in the Residence, President Clinton preferred to work in the Oval Office, often late into the night and on weekends.

This full-scale replica is identical in every detail to the Oval Office during President Clinton's years at the White House.

ft: President Clinton at work behind his desk in the Oval Office.
bove: View of the full-scale replica in the Clinton Library.

America's diversity has always been one of its greatest strengths. It is the principle embodied in the motto of the Great Seal of the United States of America: *E pluribus unum*. Out of many, one.

For President Clinton, this was more than a motto. He believed there was nothing more powerful than a diverse group of Americans working toward a common purpose. The members of his White House staff truly comprised a cross section of American life. They "looked like America" and came from many backgrounds and professions: Nobel economists, business leaders, law professors, historians, scientists, and civil rights activists. Together, they engaged in a vigorous exchange of ideas, generating innovative solutions to America's biggest challenges.

The White House at Work

ft: At work in the White House. Above: Some of the hundreds of staffers
over 30 White House offices. Left to right, row 1: Press Secretary; Chief
Staff; Management and Budget; National AIDS Policy; Advance; Cabinet
airs. Row 2: Domestic Policy Council; Staff Secretary; Public Liaison;

Legislative Affairs; Initiative for One America; Presidential Personnel.
Row 3: Oval Office Operations; Science and Technology Policy; Political
Affairs; US Trade Representative; Special Envoy for the Americas; National
Economic Council. Row 4: Presidential Scheduling; Intergovernmental

Affairs; Council on Environmental Quality; Vice President; First Lady;
Communications. Row 5: Council of Economic Advisers; Environmental
Initiatives; National Drug Control Policy; Management and Administration;
Counsel to the President; National Security Council.

THE ARCHIVES

View towards the Archives where most of the collection
is stored. The offices of the National Archives and Records
Administration (NARA) are at the far end.

A section of the climate-controlled documents archive.
More than 78 million pages of documents are stored here.

THE ARCHIVES PRESERVING THE PAST, INFORMING THE FUTURE

The Clinton Library—in fact all presidential libraries—originated under the aegis of the National Archives and Records Administration to fulfill their mission to preserve the documents and artifacts of each presidency. Historically, these archives have been called presidential libraries, but they are different from the traditional lending libraries that most Americans know in their communities. Instead, they are repositories—places where all the records and historical materials of a presidency are kept so that future scholars and everyday citizens may consult these primary sources of America's rich and complex past.

By law, every paper, email, photo, and video or recording that an administration creates or receives becomes the property of the federal government and the people of the United States. Likewise, every official gift to the president—from the drawings of a grade school class to a priceless antique presented by a visiting head of state— are also the property of the American people. Some are of great historical interest and some are merely interesting or amusing. The job of the National Archives is not to judge what future generations may wish to see or what they will find important but, rather, to ensure that they will be securely housed and catalogued so that they will always be available to an informed citizenry.

In the last days before leaving office in January 2001,
the President reviews a few remaining items to be packed up.

oving walls and racks are used to store all the objects
he collection that are not on view in the Museum.

"People are attached to the presidency in a special personal way. Their gifts and memorabilia are often like those you would present to a family member. Through this treasure trove of objects we have a true slice of late 20th century Americana. It reflects what the American people were thinking about on subjects great and small during the Clinton years."

—CHRISTINE MOUW, CURATOR

As in every other area of modern society, the volume of information and materials associated with any presidency increases with every administration. After 60 years archivists are still reviewing and releasing records from the administration of Franklin D. Roosevelt. The Clinton Presidency generated more records and artifacts than any other administration. This is partly because any two-term presidency naturally generates at least twice as much material as a single term president. Also by virtue of the evolution of information technology the Clinton Administration, as the first presidency of the Internet era, created and received millions of e-mails and generated many millions more photocopies and images.

Many of the most interesting and educational items and documents in the collection are on display in the Museum adjoining the Archives, but they represent only a small percentage of the actual material, the bulk of which is housed in climate- and humidity-controlled storage facilities in the Archives. Part of the job of the archivists is to use the latest preservation technology so that future students, scholars, and interested citizens will be able to consult these historical materials. Archivists, according to strict guidelines and laws, make records available to the public. These records can then be retrieved for researchers in the Research Room. Through the Freedom of Information Act, individuals may also submit requests for records, photographs, or other video material that have not yet been released.

The mission of preservation of our past and access to its historical record are vital to the evolution of our democracy because it is only through understanding the past that we can learn from our mistakes and build on our achievements in the future.

Eight percent of the collection is stored in over five thousand special archive boxes that are on display in the main exhibit hall.

itors study documents in the Research Room.

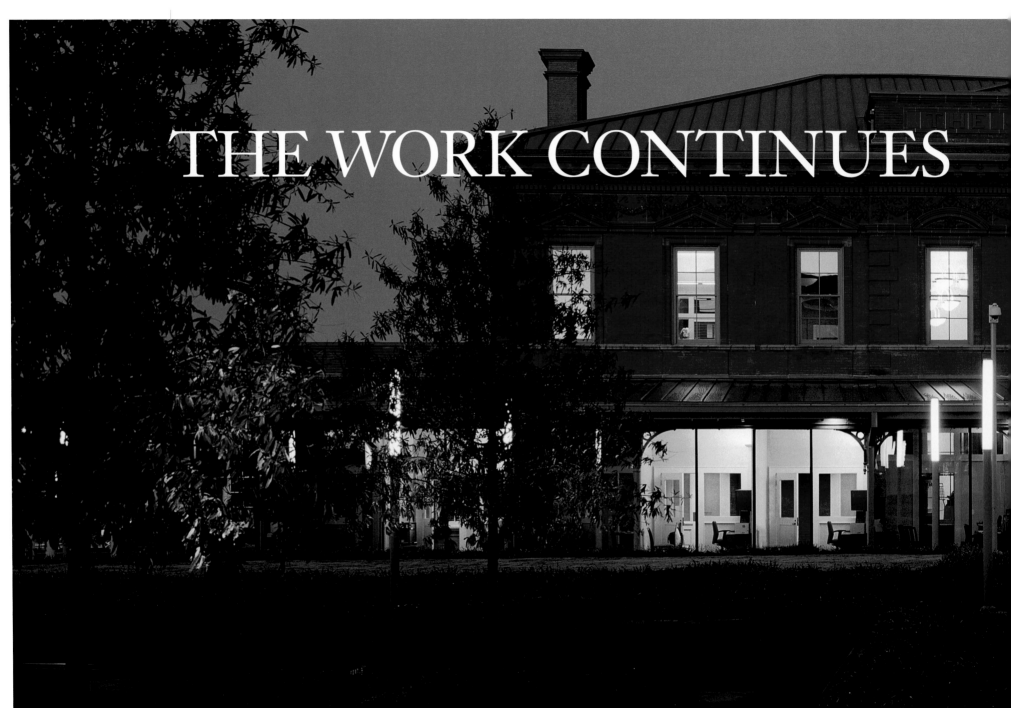

THE WORK CONTINUES

Formerly a train station on the Choctaw Route, this 19th century
building now contains the offices of the Clinton Foundation and the
University of Arkansas Clinton School of Public Service.

President Clinton speaks at the summation
of the first Clinton Global Initiative.

THE WORK CONTINUES

MOVING FROM POWER TO INFLUENCE

President Clinton left office with immense international prestige coupled with a lifelong desire to improve the lives of ordinary people, both at home and around the world. He was eager to continue his life's mission of public service. With the same energy and enthusiasm that had propelled him to the presidency, he embarked on a transition from a position of great power to a position of worldwide influence. Through the William J. Clinton Foundation, he has been able to leverage his moral force and leadership abilities and bring them to bear on the major issues of our era.

The Foundation, with offices in Little Rock and New York City, represents President Clinton's core values and the practical lessons of his experience. To pass these values and lessons onto the next generation he also joined with the University of Arkansas to establish the University of Arkansas Clinton School of Public Service, the first graduate program to grant an advanced degree in public service.

As issues facing humanity became more globalized, President Clinton realized that, through the Clinton Foundation, a new approach to problem-solving could be developed—one that made it possible to move past national borders to create an alliance of individuals and institutions of all kinds. This alliance includes individuals,

The Clinton Foundation
A New Model for a New Era

governments and non-governmental organizations (NGOs), universities, small businesses, and multinational corporations. Pooling the resources of all of these groups has allowed the Clinton Foundation to focus on clear goals that address the most challenging issues of our times in the most responsive, flexible, and effective ways. It has also enabled President Clinton to use his influence and his international stature to promote the causes that have motivated him throughout all of his years in public life.

The Clinton Foundation began its work by concentrating its efforts in four key areas: helping to alleviate poverty and promote health security; promoting effective governance; promoting racial, religious, and ethnic reconciliation; and protecting the environment. The Clinton Foundation has begun addressing this broad spectrum of issues in the United States and all over the world through a number of initiatives:

The *Clinton Foundation HIV/AIDS Initiative* (CHAI) has brought care and treatment to hundreds of thousands in the Caribbean, Latin America, Eastern Europe, Africa, and Asia. Through its agreement with manufacturers, CHAI has dramatically cut the cost of AIDS medications in the developing world. CHAI also serves as the implementing partner for the sourcing and distribution of pediatric and second-line AIDS drugs for UNITAID, a multinational fund

that will facilitate access to AIDS, malaria, and tuberculosis drugs in the developing world.

In the United States, President Clinton has addressed another health crisis: childhood obesity. The Clinton Foundation and the American Heart Association are partners in the *Alliance for a Healthier Generation* which has negotiated agreements with the soft drink industry and the nation's leading food manufacturers. The goal is to reduce the number of calories and increase the nutritional value of drinks and snack foods sold to nearly 35 million public schools students. The Alliance is also working with media partners to encourage young people to lead healthier lives through diet and exercise.

The *Urban Enterprise Initiative* provides small businesses with technical assistance and strategic advice. To advance these

...sident Clinton is greeted by children in Rwanda, 2006. On this trip, President Clinton
...eled to seven African countries to bring attention to the Clinton Foundation HIV/AIDS Initiative,
...d to visit with patients receiving treatment through Clinton Foundation programs.

Top: The President at CGI 2005, which resulted in nearly 300 commitments worth more than $2.5 billion. Bottom: At an event for the Alliance for a Healthier Generation, formed to address childhood obesity and to inspire all young Americans to develop lifelong healthy habits.

Top: In Addis Ababa, Ethiopia, President Clinton greets Jonah, a recipient of Clinton Foundation ARV medicine, as his father looks on; Bottom: Leading a discussion with graduate students at the University of Arkansas Clinton School of Public Service.

Passing the Torch

goals, the Initiative has assembled pro bono consulting teams of professionals and business students who carry out long-term assessments of small businesses to help them create practical strategies. The Initiative's *Emerging Entrepreneurs Program* (a partnership with *INC. Magazine*) supports promising business people through mentoring relationships with established entrepreneurs.

The *Clinton Global Initiative* (CGI) has brought together a wide-ranging community of global leaders to address some of the world's most pressing problems. The CGI meeting held each year in September is a vital gathering of current and former heads of state along with hundreds of other leaders from governments, the business community, and NGOs. CGI requires each participant to make a commitment to take specific action. Ongoing commitments are then monitored by the Initiative's year-round staff.

Recognizing that public health and economic growth cannot be separated from a healthy environment, the Foundation's *Clinton Climate Initiative* (CCI) is dedicated to reducing greenhouse gas emission and increasing energy efficiency by using the same business-oriented approach that has brought success to other Clinton Foundation initiatives. CCI has joined with the Large Cities Climate Leadership Group (an organization comprised of many of the world's largest cities), to create a purchasing consortium that lowers prices and aids the development of energy-saving products and assisting these cities to create programs to reduce emissions of greenhouse gases.

The Foundation is constantly expanding its scope to meet the growing challenges of our interdependent world. Learn more about the work and programs of the Clinton Foundation at www.clintonfoundation.org.

Looking back over his lifetime as a public servant, President Clinton was well aware that he had benefited time and again from the example and often the mentoring of people who had transformed their ideals into hard-won accomplishments. From the inspiration of John F. Kennedy's call to public service to the powerful orations of Martin Luther King Jr. to J. William Fulbright's pragmatic and visionary approach to international cooperation, Bill Clinton learned from the experiences of those who came before him. When he left office, one of his first priorities was to help establish the University of Arkansas Clinton School of Public Service. It will offer succeeding generations a comprehensive course of study and practical fieldwork in the nation's first program to award a Master's degree in Public Service.

The school is housed on the first floor of the historic Choctaw Building, in Sturgis Hall.

"Everyone involved, all of my classmates, took a leap of faith in a course of study that has never been done before. There is no other school that can take an attorney, a doctor, a nurse, or a teacher and give them these unique skills to serve. We really come here wanting to change the world and leave thinking we can."

—SCOTT CURRAN, CLINTON SCHOOL FOR PUBLIC SERVICE CLASS OF '06

The Hall was named in recognition of the generous bequest of the Roy and Christine Sturgis Charitable and Educational Trust. Whether students plan to pursue elective office or work for the public interest with non-profit organizations, international groups, or any level of government, the Clinton School of Public Service offers an intensive, results-oriented training ground for a new era in public service. The student body is chosen from a highly competitive field and most degree candidates come to the school with an average of two years of "real world" experience in public service. Their backgrounds vary from AmeriCorps and Peace Corps service to elementary school teaching, law, and journalism.

The classroom program is a multi-disciplinary mix of coursework, seminars, and discussions. In addition to President Clinton, the school has attracted an illustrious roster of guest lecturers including Supreme Court Justice Stephen Breyer, former Secretaries of State Henry Kissinger and Madeline Albright, Senators Bob Dole and John Edwards, Congressman John Lewis, former Vice President Dan Quayle, Historian John Hope Franklin, and Presidents José Maria Aznar of Spain and Paul Kagame of Rwanda.

The guiding principle of the program is that, at every step of their development, students immerse themselves in the real work of the most outstanding service organizations at home and abroad so that they can develop both the expertise as well as the interpersonal skills necessary to bring about change. There is a strong emphasis on developing practical skills in the field through group, individual, and international projects. The group projects have included a broad effort to stimulate growth, encourage opportunity, and attract visitors to the Mississippi Delta region. International projects have ranged from sustainable agriculture programs in Sri Lanka to community development and education in Calcutta, creating opportunities for the disabled in Vietnam, and assisting in the drafting of a new constitution for Bolivia.

This combination of a unique curriculum, interaction with leaders whose accomplishments qualify them as special teachers and mentors, and real world experience will enable every graduate to channel a strong desire to help into the reality of measurable and tangible service.

The reading room at the University of Arkansas
Clinton School of Public Service.

ARKANSAS TRAVELER

FOLLOWING THE CLINTON TRAIL

Bill Clinton was a product of a certain place in a certain era. For the most part that place was the State of Arkansas in the years between the end of the Second World War and the beginning of his Presidency. If you are visiting the Clinton Center and would like to see the places in Arkansas that had the greatest significance in Bill Clinton's life, the following destinations will give you insight into his background, as well as first hand-experience of a beautiful and historically rich part of the American heartland.

Bill Clinton during his boyhood days in Arkansas.

Little Rock

Where Bill Clinton served as governor for 12 years and where the Clintons lived from 1976 until the move to the White House.

The Clinton's first Little Rock home
(5419 L St.) The Clintons lived here while he served as attorney general from 1977-1979. Now a private residence.

The Clinton's former home
(816 Midland) The Clintons' home after he was defeated in his re-election bid for governor. Now a private residence.

The Arkansas State Capitol
(Capitol Street) Modeled after the U.S. Capitol, this is where he served as governor from 1979-1981 and from 1983-1992.

The Old Gazette Building
(112 W. Third St.) Campaign headquarters during the 1992 presidential election.

The Governor's Mansion
(18th & Center Sts.) The Clintons lived in this colonial revival mansion for 12 years.

Bronze bust of Clinton
(on the grounds of the Governor's Mansion, 18th & Center Sts.)

The Old State House
(300 W. Markham St.) On Oct. 3, 1991, Governor Clinton announced his bid for the presidency at this site. Thirteen months later, he delivered his acceptance speech in the same place. In 1996, he returned to celebrate his re-election to a second term. The Old State House served as Arkansas's first State Capitol and is now a museum of Arkansas history.

Hope

Where Bill Clinton was born and where he and his family lived for six years.

President Clinton's first home
117 S. Hervey St. Now the Clinton Birthplace Foundation) Bill Clinton lived here with his grandparents from 1946-1950.
870) 777-4455, www.clintonbirthplace.org

Second home
321 E. 13th St.) He lived here from 1950-1953 with his mother and stepfather, Roger Clinton.

The Hope Visitor Center and Museum
South Main & Division Sts., in the former Union Pacific Railroad Depot) Exhibits on the history and President Clinton's connection to Hope.
870) 722-2580, www.southwestarkansas.com

Rose Hill Cemetery
off Arkansas Highway 29) Where President Clinton's mother Virginia Kelley is buried.

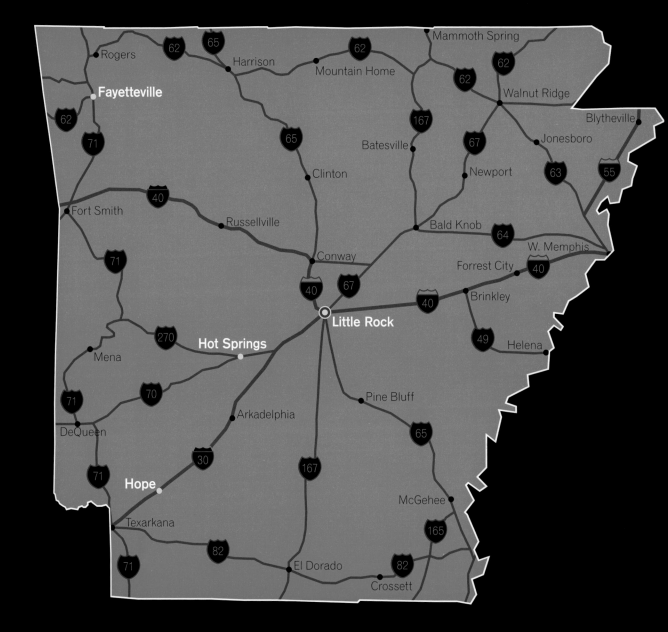

Hot Springs

Where Bill Clinton moved in 1953 and attended St. John's Catholic School, Ramble Elementary School and Hot Springs High School.

Boyhood home
(1011 Park Ave.) He and his family lived here from 1954-1961.

Park Place Baptist Church
(721 Park Ave.) Where he attended services.

View from West Mountain overlook
(Hot Springs National Park) A favorite spot for Bill Clinton and his friends.

Second Hot Springs home
(213 Scully St.) The Clinton's home from 1961 until he left for Georgetown University in 1964.

The old Hot Springs High School
(215 Oak St.) The high school he attended and graduated from in 1964.

Fayetteville

Where Bill Clinton taught at the University of Arkansas Law School, and where he began his political career.

Waterman Hall
(University of Arkansas) Home of the University of Arkansas Law School, where he taught constitutional law from 1973-1976. Hillary Rodham Clinton also taught law here.

The Clinton's former home
(930 California Blvd. Now the Clinton House Museum) The Clinton's home while in Fayetteville; their wedding took place here in October of 1975.
(877) 245-6445, www.clintonhousemuseum.com

Former Clinton campaign headquarters
(824 N. College Ave.) The office from which he launched his unsuccessful campaign to unseat U.S. Rep. John Paul Hammerschmidt.

The Presidential Library System

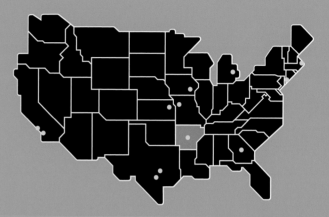

Presidential libraries can be found across the country and are as different as the leaders they honor. Every one of them presents a fascinating portrait of the country at a particular time and of the man who rose to lead it. Visit the National Archives Presidential Library website (www.archives.gov/presidential-libraries) for more information.

Herbert Hoover Library West Branch, Iowa
Franklin D. Roosevelt Library Hyde Park, New York
Harry S. Truman Library Independence, Missouri
Dwight D. Eisenhower Library Abilene, Kansas
John F. Kennedy Library Boston, Massachusetts
Lyndon B. Johnson Library Austin, Texas
Richard M. Nixon Library Yorba Linda, California
Gerald R. Ford Library Grand Rapids, Michigan
Jimmy Carter Library Atlanta, Georgia
Ronald Reagan Library Simi Valley, California
George Bush Library College Station, Texas
William J. Clinton Library Little Rock, Arkansas

Recognition

President Clinton and the William J. Clinton Foundation recognize the following individuals who participated in the construction and dedication of the William J. Clinton Presidential Center and Park.

A

Bernardo Abait
Mitchel Abbott
Brad Abercrombie
Valerie Abrams
Wendy Abrams
Chris Adams
Derrick Adams
James Adams
Josh Adams
Larry Adams
Samantha Adams
Robert Addie
Ayodele Agebede
Sebastian Aguilar
Aurelio Aguilar
Chris Ahne
Jennifer Ahne
Charles Aitkens
Greg Albanis
Ian Alberg
Mike Alberson
Austin Aldridge
Mike Alexander
Calvin Alford
Alex Allen
Glenn Allen
Jerry Allen
John Allen
Lucile Allen
Robert Allen
Jason Alley
Malcolm Allinder
Robin Allmendinger
Heather Allmendinger
David Alsobrook
Cecil Alwerdt
Brenda Anders
Dave Anderson
David Andrews
Kevin Andrews
Sam Andrews
Charles Angelier
Christine Anglin
Richard Anglin
Jimmy Anthony
Ralph Appelbaum
Frank Aquino
Jeyson Araujo
George Arendt
Debra Armack
Charles Arnett
Alexis Arnoldi
Tracy Ashcraft
Michael Ashcraft
Lori Ashworth
Richard Ashworth
Adrian Astorga
Moose Atib
Lance Atkins
Matt Atkins
Harlan Atwell
Julius Ault
Kelly Aunspaugh
Mike Aunspaugh
Mike Aurelio
Glenn Autry
Enrique Avalos
Samuel Avery
Ricky Avilez-Pena
Joseph Axalson
Joseph Axelson

B

Kimberly Babb
Randy Babb
LeRoy Backus
Carla Backus
Ronnie Bagley
Susan Bailey
Bill Bailey
Leroy Bailey

Richard Bailey
Edward Bailey, Jr.
Bryan Baker
Brian Baker
Sherrie Baker
Andrew Baker
Roger Baker
Jason Baker
Billy Ball
Mark Ballheimer
Bill Ballint
L.T. Baltimore
Doug Band
Billy Banister
Jimmy Banister
Rick Banks
Otis Banks
Julie Bannon
Dan Baranek
Everett Barentine
David Barger
Danny Barger
Dennis Barnaby
David Barnes
Farolyn Barnett
Michael Barnwell
Joe Barthol
Martin Bartolomundo
Don Basinger
Michael Bass
Dal Batchelder
Brad Batchleor
Jerry Bates
Callie Bates
Charles Batson
David Batts
Christena Baugh
Jean Bauman
Noy Bayani
Garry Bearden
James Beatty
Vernon Beauchamp
Ben Beaumont
Melissa Beavers
Carolyn Beck
Julie Becker
Angie Beckwith
Martin Beggs
Ed Bell
Don Belliveau
Rene Beltran
Robert Bendigo
L. James Benedick
Katie Benish
Felix Benitz
Danny Bennett
Derrel Bennett
Stacy Bennett
Leslie Benningfield
Gene Benson
Paul Benson
Jeff Bentley
Ronnie Benton
Adam Bergfeld
Lindsey Berman
Bonnie Berry
Isable Besa
Elias Besa
Francesca Bettridge
Edward Bevill
Subra Bhat
Anmol Bhatia
Raymond Bialkowski
Jeff Biggerstaff
Javier Bile
John Billera
Michael Billings
Brenda Billingsley
Dan Billingsley
Carlton Billingsley
Kim Billingsley
David Billiott

Danny Binz
John Binz
Lee Ann Binz
Philip Binz
Steve Binz
Terry Binz
Victor Birch
Victor Birch
Lynn Birkett
Brian Bisgood
Lisa Bishop
Eugenie Bisulco
Ed Bitter
Adrianna Bitter
Robert Bitter
Bobby Blacklock
Leslie Blacklock
Blue Blair
Greg Blair
Nevis Blanchard
Maurice Bland
Billy Blasingame
Francis Blasingame
Chris Blaylock
Eric Blaylock
Charles Blessing
Adam Blight
Tracy Blood
Josh Blumenfeld
Keith Bly
Barry Bobbitt
Christopher Bobbitt
John Bochiechio
Elizabeth Boddington
Nicole Boddington
Tim Boe
Jeff Boehm
Victor Bogard
Ike Bogard
Kenneth Bolton
Thomas Bolton
Amy Bonitatibus
Anthony Book
Felton Booker
Christopher Books
William Booth
Michael Boothe
Chris Borgens
Chris Borne
Mark Borton
Teri Borton
Curtis Boulanger
Rodney Bounds
Jonathan Bourne
Gwen Bowen
Curtis Boyce
Derek Boyce
Charles Boyd
Sam Boyd
Marcus Boyd
Jimmy Boyer
John Boyer
Chet Boyette
Drew Boyles
Brad Boyles
Nathan Bozer
Joseph Brackett
Jay Bradford
Ron Bradford
John Bradley
Barry Brady
Benjamin Brady
Garry Brand
James R. Brand
Neal Braningan
Jack Brannon III
Kay Branton
Larry Breeding
Ronny Breeding
Preston Breeding
Darryl Breen
Chris Breshers

Carl Brickey
Nick Brimhall
Bruce Brock
Matthew Brockmon
Gretchen Brodtman
Sheila Bronfman
Bethany Brookings-Semans
Ronnie Brooks
Anthony Brooks
Chris Brown
Randall Brown
Robert Brown
Shirley Brown
Doug Brown
Greg Brown
Gary Brown
Tony Brown
Sandy Brown
Cynthia Brown
Paul Brown
Justin Brown
Kim Brown
Robert Brownell
Boyce Browning
Steven Browning
Denise Browning
Penny Brrimhall
Guy Bruce
Travis Bruchfield
Jim Brunson
Darrell Bryant
Phillip Bryant, Jr.
Phillip Bryant, Sr.
Sue Buchanan
Eric Buck
Ken Buck
Bruce Bulpitt
Edward Bunche, Jr.
Karen Burchard
Craig Burchfield
Michael Burd
Jim Burford
Gary Burford
Sherry Burgener
Benjamin Burgess
Marsha Burgess
Donald Burkholder
Troy Burleson
Rodney Burns
Elmer Burns
Michael Burns
Kevin Burns
Kenny Burroughs
Lee Burrows
Chris Burrows
Stace Burruss
Terry Burruss
George Burt
Andru Bush
Deborah Bush
Randal Bush
Debra Butler
Kyle Butler
Shannon Butler
Dean Byrd
Mary Beth Byrne

C

Fe Fe Cabe
Delfino Cabrera
Ronnie Cagle
Benito Calera
Alejandro Calletano
Larry Callison
Trennis Campbell
Pamela Campbell
Shane Campbell
Caroline Campbell
Jimmy Campbell
Ricardo Candel
Neto Canisales

Juan Cano
Ricardo Cano
Kevin Canterbury
Guy Caple
Wallace Caradine
Ashley Caradine
Carmine Carannante
Neith Cardenas
Billy Carey
Charles Carloss
David Carlton
Carolyn Carlton
Don Carpenter
Manuel Carrasco
Kirk Carrie
Jorge Carrillo
Shawn Carroll
Dylan Carroll
George Carroll
Lindsy Carson
Kevin Carter
Glen Carter
Doni Carter
Robert Carter
Carolyn Carter
Jeff Carter
Chris Carter
George Carter, Jr.
Chris Cary
Danny Casey
Joe Cashion
Steve Castagno
Gonzalo Castaneda
Jose Castanon
Ernesto Castelan
Elaine Castellano
Vincent Castiglia
Joseph Castille
Ricardo Castillo
Hipolito Castilo
Chris Castleberry
J. H. Castleberry
Marvin Castleberry
Ricky Castleberry
Micheal Cathcart
Clinton Caudle
Charles Caudle, Jr
Charles Caudle, Sr
Mike Cearley
Jose Cedillos
Augustine Cerna
David Chadick
Jenifer Chadwick
Alyson Chadwick
Glenn Chalmers
Leann Chambers
Julia Couch
Cathy Chan
Tanya Chan
Barry Chaney
Debra Chappell
Stephen Charla
Edgar Chavajay
George Cheramie
Melissa Chester-Letendre
Abb Childers
Romie Childers, Jr.
Aaron Craig
Neal Childs
John Chizmadia
Tony Chors
Mary Chrisman
Laury Christensen
Ron Christensen
Scott Christiaens
Anthony Christian
Heather Christian
Heidi Christian
Andrew Chymarzewski
Hilario Cisneros
James Cissell
Carolyn Claeys
Sean Clair

Timothy Clark
Dave Clark
Mark Clark
Travis Clark
James Clark
Robert Clark
Tahira Clarke
Corey Clayton
Chris Clement
Lindsey Clements
Grant Clements
Donald Clements
Raymond Clements
Debbie Clements
Luke Cline
Tim Cloclough
Remont Cobb
Daryl Coburn
Don Cochran
Aaron Colclough
Coleman Coleburn
Paul Coleman
William Coleman
Jerry Coleman
Tony Coles
David Collie
Lee Collier
Sean Collins
Carmen Comer
Bobby Conder
Walter Conley, Jr.
AnnMaura Connolly
Juan Contreras-Gonzales
Buddy Cook
Lowell Cook
Jeremy Cook
Jason Cooper
Andrew Cooper
Janie Cooper
Clint Cooper
Justin Cooper
Trey Copeland
Grover Corbell
Timeo Cordadini
Robert Cordell
Wayne Cornish
Brian Corrigan
Adalberto Cortez
James Cortina
Mary Cortina
Joseph Cortina
Gary Corum
Marjorie Corum
Amelia Costigan
Julia Couch
John Coulter
Chris Courson
Rick Cowan
Joseph Cowin
Joey Cox
Dwight Cox
Benny Cox
John Cox
David Cox
David Craddock
Aaron Craig
Kelly Craighead
Will Cranston
Scott Craven
Kevin Creasey
Tim Creed
Milton Crews
Anna Crider
David Crites
Gary Crittenden
Katherine Crowley
Philip Crowley
Crisoforo Cruz
Carrie Cruze
Roberto Cuarezma
Jesse Cuclager

Robert Cunningham
Betty Currie
Ramon Curtis
Kate Cury
Kieran Cusack

D

Ronda Dailey
Roy Dale Cox
Isaac Dale, Jr
Boddy Dalton
Joe Dalton
Kathryn Daniel
Kenneth Daniel
Eddie Daniels
Sherri Daniels
Kirk Danielson
Ross Darby
Terry Davenport
Jeffery Davenport
Steve Davidson
James Davis
James Davis
Scott Davis
Mark Davis
Charlie Davis
Sean Davis
James Davis
Thomas Davis
Angela Davis
Rose Davis
Allen Davis
Ben Davis
Elizabeth Daw
Nakia Dawkins
Calvin Day
Martin Day
Roosevelt Day
Nancy Dayhoff
Kevin De Vorak
Paul Dean
Aaron DeBoer
Melissa Decker
Russell Declements, Jr.
Simone DeFelice
Dan DeFossey
Eileen DeGuzman
Miguel Delgado
Jerry Delong
Joseph DelPozzo
Steve Deluna
Matt Demo
Steve Dennis
John Denton
Tyler Denton
Stephen DePriest
John Deramus
Joseph Deuerling
Michael Deuerling
Nicholas Devlin
Nealon DeVore
Terry Devton
Dexter Doyne
Emmanuel Diascosavvas
Martin Diaz
Javier Diaz
Jose Diaz
Jose Diaz Lopez
Martin Diaz Lopez
David Dickens
W. Keith Dickerson
Phyllis Dickerson
M. Jane Dickey
Robyn Dickey
Brian Didier
Robert Digby
William Dillard
Richard Dillavou
James Dirks
Joey Dixon

Lynda Dixon
Jennifer Doherty
Dennis Dollar
Joe Dollarhide
James Dorrell
Keith Dorsey
William Doty
Grover Doughty
James Douglas
Mark Dove
Tim Downing
Peter Doyle
Roger Doyne
Greg Dozier
Charles Draper
Danny Draper
Tony Draper
Seth Draper
Cinde Drilling
Earnest Duckery
Herman Duckworth Jr.
David Duerr
Lance Dulaney
John Dunaway III
Gerald Duncan
Michelle Durpetti
Lou Dutton
Bobby Dycus
Troy Dye
Justin Dyer

E

Mike Eady
Ronnie Eagle
Olivia Easterling
John Easterwood
Louis Easterwood
David Echols
Gina Eddy
Deborah Edelstein
Anne Edwards
Butch Edwards
Kathy Edwards
Shane Edwards
Thomas Edwards
Barbara Eggleston
Richard Ehlen
Beth Ehrhardt
Heidi Eikenhorst
Gary Eikenhorst
Cathy Eikenhorst
Newton Elder
Solomon Eljashev
Michael Ellenburg
David Ellis
David Ellis
Blake Elmore
Daniel Embry
Jeanette Emery
Judith Engelken
Larry Engels
Larry England
Curt England
Fred English
Jeremy Enloe
Josh Enloe
Tina Eoff
Odes Epperson
Dale Epting
Bob Ernspiker
Stanley Ervin
Rudy Escobedo
Selvin Escobedo
Adolfo Escobedo
Michael Eskra
Felipe Esparza-Sustayta
Juan Espinoza
Misael Espinoza
Vicente Espinoza
Tommy Ethridge
Tony Eubanks
Dan Euser

Gary Evans
Don Evans
Sharon Evans
Michael Evans, Jr.
Michael Evans, Sr.
Angela Exposito

F

Connie Fails
Tutty Fairbanks
Blas Fajardo
Alvin Farmer
Khalilah Farmer
Sharon Farmer
Sarah Farnsworth
Lindsay Farr
Theodore Farrand
William Faschan
John Faulkner
Maria Favata
Steve Feder
Myra Fein
Frederick Fells
Mark Fenley
Justin Fenton
Tricia Fenton
Douglas Ferebee
Jorge Fernandez
Emma Fernandez
Al Fernandez
Justin Ferren
David Ferren
Susan Ferriel
Marco Fierro
Hans Fifer
Curtis Finley
Craig Fischer
Michaela Fitzhugh
Randy Flakes
Joseph Fleischer
Kevin Fleming
Herb Flemming
Darrell Flemmons
John Fletcher
Dave Flood
Ruben Flores
Pedro Flores
Oscar Flores
Ronald Flowers
Gene Fluker
James Fohn
Tom Foley
Dan Foley
Danny Folsom
Bruce Folsom
William Forbess
Brian Ford
Stephen Ford
James Ford
Dale Forrest
Hershel Forrester
Scott Fortenberry
Mark Fortier
Gary Foulk
Paul Fowler
Mike Fox
Ed Fraiser
Bill Franks
David Frazee
Ted Frederich
Keena Freeman
John Freeman
William French
Jonathan French
Mary French
Guy Fronte
Michael Frost
James Fryer
Donna Fulghum
Brad Fuller
John Fultz
David Furlos

G

Dennis Gaffney
Larry Gaines
Jaret Gaither
Homero Galica
Julio Gallegos
David Gallegos
Claire Galloway
Terry Gambill
Pam Gangluff
Elisha Gant
Sean Garber
Jose Garcia
Bacilio Garcia
Pedro Garcia
Manuel Garcia
Jorge Garcia
Otoniel Garcia
Nelson Garcia
Socimo Garcie
Craig Gardner
Constantino
  Garduno
Raul Garduno
Richard Garlock
William Garrett
Josh Garrett
Jamie Gartman
Charlie Gaston
Charlie Gaston
Gary Gately
Melody Gately
Mark Gates
Curtis Gattis
Timothy Geary
Sarah Gegenheimer
Eric Geier
Dan Genshaft
Gary Gentry
Jody Gentry
R. Alan Gentry
Robert George
Bobby George
Angelia George
Janell George
Alice Gerhart
Harvey Gershman
Elizabeth Gibson
Daryl Gilbert
Joseph Gilbert
Archie Giles
Kamni Gill
Linda Gillam-Weir
Kathy Gillespie
Neil Gillespie
Kelly Gillihan
Michael Gilliland
Bill Ginalick
Dawn Giovanini
Ezell Girley
Che' T Givens
Travas Givens
Alfonzo Givens
Kathryn Glass
Ronnie Glover
Laurie Goldberg
Ross Goldstein
Guillermo Gomez
Luiz Gomez
Louis Gonyea
Altemar Gonzalez
Douglas Gonzalez
Armando Gonzalez
Ronald Good
Heather Goodman
Herman Goodman
Charles Goodman, Jr
Rick Goodrum
Karen Gorczyca
Daniel Gordon
Greg Gore
Dennis Gorrell

Tommy Goss
Mitchell Gough
Edward Grace
Matthew Grage
Regina Graham
Jonathan Graham
Rossi Graham
Laura Graham
Dru Graves
Roger Gravis
Michael Gray
Dave Greelish
Bryan Green
John Green
Clevester Green
David Green
Donnie Green
David Green
David Green
David Green
Earl Green
Bern Green
Charles Green
Don Green
Nancy Green
Lamar Green
Ed Greening
Stephen Greenlee
Clifton Gregory
Steve Gregory
James Gregory
Jessen Gregory
Donald Greis
Rodney Greis
Otis Griffin
Gary Griffis
Brad Groff
Falone Gross
Marc Gross
John Grubb
Roberto Gualajara
Ramon Guardiola
James Guenther
Danny Guffey
Carl Guinesso, Jr.
Shanan Guinn
Onur Gulec
Mark Gunderman
Jack Gunter
Ed Gunther
Greg Gunther
John Gunther
Ronald Guthrie
Jose Gutierrez
Freddy Gutierrez
David Gutierrez
Sabino Gutierrez

H

Robert Haak
Donnie Hager
William Hahn
Billy Hailey
William Halbert
Karl Halcolmb
Gene Hale
Robert Hale
Greg Hale
Kevin Haley
Mark Hall
Lonnie Hall
Mark Hall
Rodney Hall
Ryan Hall
Gretchen Hall
Knoxie Hall, Jr.
Belinda Halliburton
Ronny Hallmark
Paul Hamilton
Tucker Hamilton
Edward Hamilton
Sarah Hamilton

Aumbray
  Hammonds, Sr.
Carl Hampel
Tim Hampel
Pat Hampel
Maurice Hampton
Bart Handford
Sally Handley
Devin Hanlin
Tom Hanlon
Glenn Hannah
David Harbin
Lucas Hargraves
George Hargreaves
Robbie Hargrove
Mike Harkey
Doyle Harlan
James Harmon
Dwight Harned
Casey Harness
Paul Harp
James Harper
Rickey Harper
Stephen Harral
Byl Harriel
Kenneth Harris
James Harris
J. T. Harris
Dewayne Harris
Gano Harris
Janet Harris
Jerry Harrison
Josh Hartley
Heath Hartman
Angela Hartman
Robert Hartwick
Grady Harvell
Alan Hassel
Wayne Hassel
Jerry Hassel
Matthew Hassel
Mariah Hatta
Donnie Haulcomb
Madge Havniear
Robert Hawkins
Gary Hawkins
Todd Hawkins
Connie Hawley
Dolly Hayden
Earl Hayes
Martin Hayes
Martin Hayes
Shaun Hayes
Jason Hayes
Ronald Haygood
Bill Haynes
Ray Hays
Teresa Healy-Bolin
Robert Hearne
Michael Hearnsburger
Richard Hearon
Patrick Heffner
Jay Heidbrink
Ryan Heiges
Rory Heinley
Tom Hejna
Brad Hemphill
Calvin Hence
Susan Henderson
George Henderson
Justin Hendricks
Mike Hendrix
Richard Hendrix
Jason Henry
Aaron Hermosillo
Joel Hermosillo
Manuel Hermosillo
Noe Hernandez
Guillermo Hernandez
Pedro Hernandez
Alfredo Hernandez
Roberto Herrera

Judd Herring
Ricky Herron
Roy Herron
Cindy Herron
James Higashi
Charlie Hill
Kenny Hill
Jerry Hill
Roger Hill
Glenn Hill
D.B. Hill III
John Hills
Jeffrey Hinmon
Joanne Hiromura
Dean Hirscheider
Cephas Hobbs
Kaki Hockersmith
Pam Hodge
Kat Hodge
Elliott Hodges
John Hodoway
Mike Hogue
Jody Holbrook
Kenneth Holeman
Brad Holicer
Brandon Holland
Shawn Hollingshead
Lannie Hollis
William Holloway
Robert Holloway
Dave Holman
Bobbie Holman
Thomas Holman
Yancy Holmes
Frank Holt
Keith Honold
Angie Hoofman
Roger Hoofman
Derick Hooie
Moses Hooks
Alan Hope
Whitney Hopper
Mike Horn
Oneka Horne
  Tolentino
Deanne Horsly
Jack Horton
Kevin Horton
Jon Horton
James Horvath
Michael Horvath
Marcus Houston
Michelle Houston
Anthony Howard
Gary Howard
Thomas Howard
William Howard III
Andy Hrivnak
Jeff Hubar
Lanny Hubbard
Christopher Hubbell
Katherine Huber
Charlie Hudson
Brandon Huffman
Gregory Hughes
John Hughes
Sean Hughes
Joe Huitt
Gary Hula
Wes Hunt
David Hunter
Brian Hurt
Geronimo Hurtado
Charles Hyden
Ryan Hymes
Ryan Hymes
Shawn Hynes

I

Adolfo Ibarra
Melanie Ide
Fausto Imperias

Brandon Inmon
John Irish
Glen Irvin

J

Katie Jack
Robert Jackson
Paul Jackson
Louis Jackson
James Jackson
Jerry Jackson
Craig Jackson
Tommy Jackson
Dwight Jackson
Earl Jackson, Jr.
Gary Jaggers
Gene James
Nathan James
Carrie James
Wenzday Jane
Lester Janiszewski
Wayne Jaques
Andrew Jaques
Aimee Jasculca
Andrew Jasculca
Judy Jasculca
Lauren Jasculca
Rick Jasculca
Ron Jefford
Floyd Jenkins, Sr.
Jerry Jennings
Thomas Jennings
Brett Jimenez
Jesus Jimenez
Christen Johansen
Gary Johnson
Derrick Johnson
Toby Johnson
Johnny Johnson
Jim Johnson
Roy Johnson
Richard Johnson
Johnny Johnson
Butch Johnson
Glyn Johnson
Ray Johnson
Tony Johnson
William Johnson
MaryBeth Johnson
Jane Johnson
Joe Johnson
Jonathan Johnson
Jordan Johnson
James Joiner
Johtel Jointer
A. Don Jolley
Roy Jones
Roderic Jones
Ben Jones
Gary Jones
Todd Jones
Chris Jones
Steve Jones
Blair Jones
Adam Jones
Richard Jones
Lance Jones
Rick Jones
Kenneth Jones
Samuel Jones
Brian Jones
Charles Jones
Terry Jones
Curtis Jones
Earl Jones
Tom Jones
Charles Jones
Jody Jones
Charles Jones
Kerry Jones
Eric Jones
Sarah Jones

L

Scott Lacey
Mark Ladov
Jean Lafleur
Steven Lafleur
Freddie Laire
Phillip Lake
Phil Lambert
Marie Lambert
James Lambert
Dale Lambright

W. Wilson Jones
Hartmut Jordan
Kenneth Jordan
Lewis Jordan
Paula Jordan
Rickey Jordan
Westley Jordan
Pascal Jouffriault
Stephen Joyce
Federico Juarez
Bobby Judkins
Sylvia Juran

K

Greg Kaiser
Ann Kamps
Rossen Karadjov
David Karnes
Mark Karnes
John Kaucher
Jerry Keane
Chris Kell
John Keller
Antwyan Kelley
Randle Kelley
Thomas Kelley
Bobby Kelley
Stephen Kelly
Eddie Keltner
Chris Keltner
Martina Kendig
Linda Kendrick
Sharon Kennedy
Jim Kennedy
Marty Kent
Timothy Keown
Johnny Kerr
Andrew Kessel
Shane Key
Jerry Kilgore
Alfred Kimbrell
John King
Sherry King
Jason King
Kimberly King
Phil Kingdon
Kevin Kinsey
Marsha Kinsman
Charles Kisner
David Klawetter Jr.
Bradley Klein
Frank Knight
Brodrick Knight
Dewayne Knight
John Locascio
Karen Lockner
Bo Loeffel
Sammie Loftis
Ray Loftis
Charlotte London
William Long
Charles Looney
Tomas Lopez
Leopoldo Lopez
Francisco Lopez
Gabriel Lopez
George Lopez
Adolfo Lopez
Alberto Lopez
Ramiro Lopez
Melecio Lopez
  Estrada
Frank Lopresti
Jason Loquet
Toni Losier
James Love
Mark Love
Sylvester Loving
Clifford Loy
Ramon Loyola
Jeannie Lucas
Mark Lucier
Sean Lucke
Jennifer Lucrezi

Irwin Lamontagne
Tom Lane
Melissa Laney
Helen Langan
Bryan Langley
Harry Langley
Mitchell Langley
Jose Lara
Connie LaRossa
Jeremiah Latimore
James Lavender
Donna Lawrence
Bobby Lawson
James Lawson
Wes Lawson
Kenneth Layton
Vince Leahy
Robert Leake
Scott Lee
Gregory Lee
Johnny Lee
Doug Lee
Seung-Je Lee
Sang Lee
Timothy Leland
Clint Lemons
Rick Lenzen
Juan Leon
Rufino Leon
Linda Leopoulos
Dwayne Lester
Chris Levart
Geoffrey Lewicke
Bradley Lewis
Mark Lewis
Randy Lewis
Justin Lewis
Glenn Lewis
Isaac Lewis
Michael Lewis
Steve Lewis
Mark Limberg
Mark Limberg
Amy Lin
David Lindow
Bruce Lindsey
Anton Lischeron
Summer Littlefield
Todd Littleton
Albert Litwa
Albert Litwa
James Lloyd
Gerald Martin

Michael Lufrano
Ramiro Luis
Fernando Lujan
Tim Luna
Marisa Luzzatto
Ray Lynch

M

Raul Macias
Jackie Mack
Don MacKinnon
Fredrick Mackey
Richard Madaglia
Matt Madden
Amy Maddox
Joseph Magner
Victor Mahan
Anthony Mahone
Robert Maisen
Ronnie Majkrzak
Juan Maldonado
Robert Malik
Mark Malin
Paul Malkie
Artemio Malpica
Earnett Maltbia
Michael Manassee
David Mankin
James Mann
Kate Mann
Stacey Mannari
Rickey Manning
Titus Manning
Vincent Marci
Gregory Margeson
Antonio Marin
Fabian Marks
Harley Marsh
Quawn Marshall
Tommy Marshall
Capricia Marshall
Ramon Martar
Walter Martin
Lamont Martin
Judith Martin
John Martin
Ron Martin
Billy Martin
LaDonna Martin
Johnny Martin
Brian Martin
Michael Martin
Gerald Martin
Miguel Martinez
Charles Martinez
Dustin Martinez
Raul Martinez
Jorge Martinez
Juan Martinez
Robert Melton
Elaine Melton
Joe Melton
John Murphy
Amelia Murphy
Larry Murray
Jack Murray
Stephen Myers
Larry Myers
Sam Myers Jr.

N

Kevin Nagle
Joe Nalley
Ron Nantze
Cris Nash
Hugo Navarro
  Gonzalez
Sergio Navarro
  Gonzalez
Antonio Navarro Rivera
Baltazar Navarro Rivera
Gary Naylor

Jesse McBride
Karl McBride
Mike McCarthy
Scott McCauley
Jon McClain
Jim McClelland
Kevin McClurkan
Trudy McCollum
Phllip McCormick
Rudy McCormick
Shawna McCormick
Dennis McDaniel
Ervin McDonald
Larry McDonald
Noel McDoniel
Justin McDougal
Glenn McElroy
Scott McElroy
Bobby McElroy
Ruth McElroy
Emily McElwain
Charles McFadden
David McFarland
Jessie McFarlin
John McFerran
Brad McGee
Bruce McGee
Debby McGinn
Paul McGlaum
Kavan McGonigal
Molly McGowan
Joe McGowen
Mark McGraw
Chad McGriff
Grady McGuire
John McKeller
Jeremy McKenzie
Dennis McKissick
Ben McLaughlin
Sonia McLean
Forrest McMillan
Robert McMillian
John McMillin
Kenneth McNeal
Aubrey McNeeley
Mary McNeill
Matthew McNerney
William McNulty
Brian McPartlin
Ronnie McQuain
Lesley McShane
Marsha McVey
Donnell Meadows
Antonio Medeiros
Bertha Medlock
David Medlock
Jimmy Medlock
Harland Melton
Julie Napear
George Ormsby
Melissa Orsini
Ivan Ortiz
Armondo Ortiz
Heron Ortiz
Donnie Osborne
Kevin Otey
Chima Otuechere
Niel Overton
Leoney Owens

P

Abner Pacheco
Kevin Pack
Johnny Pak
George Pak
Ole Palludan
Randolph Palmer
Victor Palos
Julie Panebianco
Edgar Papazian
Alejandro Parades
Miguel Parades

Larry Miller
Billy Miller
Loye Miller
Clay Miller
Catherine Miller
Robert Miller
Carnie Miller
Megan Miller
T.J. Miller
Billy Miller
Nacoma Miller
Charlie Newcomb
Casey Newton
Clarence Nice
DeeDee Nicholas
Robert Nichols
Robert Nichols
Brin Nirenberg
Timothy Nixon
John Noble
Eric Nonacs
Ron Norby
Kevin Norman
Tracy Norman
Jeremy Norman
John Normolye
John Norwood
James Norwood
Cecil Norwood
Gerald Norwood, Jr.
Gerald Norwood, Sr.
Joe Nowlin
Terry Nowlin
Gary Nutt
Dewayne Nutter

O

Chris O'Cain
Kevin O'Connor
Brian O'Connor
Patrick O'Connor
Wes O'Donohue
Tanya O'Donohue
David O'Halloran
Peter O'Keefe
Tucker O'Neal
Brandon Oakley
Leonardo Ochoa
Dean Odom
Clinton Oglesby
Brian Oherron
John Ohmnacht
Richard Olcott
Fernando Oliveira
Ernest Oliver
Philip Oliver
Audra Oliver
Fernando Oliveria
Adolfo Ordonez
Ronnie Neal
Matthew Nellums
Michael Nelson
Jerime Nelson
Brad Nelson
Bryan Nelson
Milton Nelson, Jr.
Milton Nelson, Sr.
David Neslen
Jeff Netto
Neal New

Michael Parchman
Scott Parker
Shadd Parker
Bobby Parker
Robert Parker
Eric Parker
Tim Parker
Earnest Parnell
Russell Parnell
Tim Parr
Daniel Parrick
Roy Parrott
Mike Parscale
Lamont Parson
John Pate
Kathleen Pate
Evelyn Patrick
David Patterson
Barry Pattillo
Philip Patton
Don Patton
Alan Payne
Travis Payne
Denver Peacock
Kelly Pearce
Bo Pearson
Sam Pease
Jason Pebley
David Pecoraro
Jim Pedigo
Tim Peeler
Timothy Peeler
David Peeler
Kenneth Peeler
Danny Peeples
Topsy Pelkey
Jose Pena
Tina Pence
James Pendley
Charley Penix
Samuel Perez
Jose Perez
Jose Perez
Moises Perez
Eduardo Perez
Elias Perez
Michael Perez
Timothy Perkins
John Perkins
Kathryn Perkins
Shannon Perkins
John Perkins, Jr
Daniel Perry
Denise Persons
Jerry Petefish
Prentiss Peters
Kinshasa Peterson
Paul Petrarca
Tony Petruzziello
Don Pettypool
David Peveto
Frank Phillippi
Jessica Phillippi
Randy Phillips
Kenneith Phillips
Eric Phillips
Adrien Phillips
Geoff Phillips
Tim Phillips
Vince Pianalto
Larry Piechocki
Eileen Pierce
Chuck Pietrowski
Saul Pinal
Juan Pinon
Miguel Pinon
Eddie Piotrowski
Billy Piper
Tolga Piskiner
Debbie Pitt
Beckey Pitt
Charmian Place

Robert Plaisance
Stephen Platenberg
Patrick Plourde
Larry Plunkett
Wally Podrazik
Stephen Poe
Kia Polee
Tommy Polk
James Polshek
Gary Pomerantz
Seth Pomeroy
Tobey Porta
David Porter
Sally Porter
Juan Portillo
Tammy Postal
Chris Poston
Thomas Potts
L. Richard Poulin
Harold Pounders
Michael Powell
Lea Prainsack
Tim Prater
Mario Precopio
Jamie Prence
Harold Prestenburg
Beverlee Prevost
Michael Price
Eric Price
Robert Price
Herbert Price
Charles Priest
Sharon Priest
Gerald Prince
Rodney Proctor
Dencie Proctor
Cindy Pruitt
Tina Puddephatt
W. John Pugh
Michael Purifoy
Dan Purtle
Jimmie Purvis
Jessica Pynoos
Kate Pynoos

Q

David Quattlebaum
Stanley Quattlebaum
Ralph Quattrucci
Todd Quick

R

Joe Raborn
Jamie Radice
Vinod Raghavan
Nathan Raines
Tonya Rainey
Cody Ralston
Daniel Ramirez
Jesus Ramirez
Nicolas Ramirez-Torres
Jose Ramos
Donald Randle
Curtis Raney
Jeff Rankin
Terry Rasco
Jereme Rasico
Shaun Rateliff
John Ratliff
Alejandro Raudales
Billy Ray
Frank Ray
Frank Ray III
Baldemar Rebollar
Bobby Record
Ricky Red
Mark Redd
Vellis Redden
Mike Redmon
Kyle Reece
Gene Reed

Wallace Reed
Vincent Reed
Susan Reedy
Alana Reeves
Michael Regan
John Reihl
Evelyn Reilly
Joe Reilly
Philippe Reines
Juan Renavato
Nila Rengstorf
Dennis Rennard
Elaine Renouf
Marco Resendiz
Shane Reynolds
Amy Reynolds
Jim Rhee
James Rhoades
Dusty Rhoads
Holly Rhode
Rodney Rhoden
Craig Rhodes
Adam Rhyne
Billy Rice
Michael Rice
Steven Richardson
Jarid Richardson
Hannah Richert
Arriana Richter
Michael Riddly
Suzie Ridgley
Blake Riegler
Conor Riffle
Marci Riggs
Leon Rios
Antonio Rios
Rodolfo Rios
Bill Ritchie
Leo Rivera
Carl Roberson
Archie Roberson
Dewayne Roberts
Jimmy Roberts
Mike Roberts
Trenity Roberts, Sr.
George Robertson
Jerry Robertson
Leslie Robertson
Everett Robinson
Keith Robinson
Lynne Robinson
Melanie Robinson
Anthony Robinson
Keith Robinson
Shannon Robinson
Keith Robinson
Glen Robinson
Keith Robinson
Helen Robinson
Taren Robinson
Emily Robison
Jeff Rochelle
Janet Rochner
Marco Rodas
Joe Roddy
Jesse Rodgers
Leonel Rodriguez
Jesus Rodriguez
Fred Rodriguez
Gerardo Rodriguez
Miguel Rodriguez
Isabelle Rodriguez
Uriel Rodriguezo
Sergio Rodriquez
George Roe
Golden Rogers
Carl Rogers
Nick Rogers
Carl Rogers, III
Ellis Rolax
Nadine Roller

Alan Romans
Jise Romero
Humberto Romero
Jose Romero
Lonnie Roncali
Greg Roofener
Dan Rook
Matt Rorex
Jorge Rosas
W.C. Ross
Tony Ross
Tom Rowat
Mary Rowe
Mario Felipe Ruano
Aaron Ruby
Mike Ruggeri
Michael Ruggeri
Jason Rundel
Tommy Runnels
Matt Runyon
Jimmy Runyon
Steve Russell
Clinton Russell
Larry Russell
Elizabeth Russell
Chris Russenberger
Skip Rutherford
Blake Rutherford
William Rutter

S

Donald Sackett
Vincent Sagart
Bob Salamone
Raphael Salas
Baltazar Salazar
Juan Salazar
Fidel Saldivar
James Sale
Ronald Saleh
David Sales
Jon Salomon
Marty Salzberg
Stephen Samford
Bradley Sample
Pia Samrithikul
Emilio Sanchez
Bradley Sanders
Carol Sanders
Tara Sanders
Butch Sanders
George Sanders
Roselyn Sanders
Miriam Sanders
Edward Sanders, Jr.
Jim Sanderson
Scott Sandlin
Kendal Sandridge
Shital Sanghaui
Antonio Santana
Jorge Santana
Vivian Santora
David Sargent
Truman Sarrels
Chetin Sarva
Paraag Sarva
Leo Sassani
Jose Saucedo
Martin Saucedo
Michael Saville
Jay Saxton
Van Saylor
Van Saylor
Debra Schiff
Nick Schmit
David Schmitt
Shane Schock
Shane Schock
Andreas Scholte
Horst Scholte
Gary Schreffler
Marianne Schuit

Laura Schwartz
Ben Schwerin
Ruel Scott
Ronnie Scott
Velleta Scott
Eddie Scott
Eric Scruggs
David Scull
Joe Searan
Tim Seaton
Kristy Sebastian
Robert Sedlak
Saw-Teen See
Keith Seelinger
Robert Seibert
Kerry Seiffert
Tim Seiter
Jonathan Semans
Scott Semple
Ed Sergeant
Daniel Sesil
Archie Seward
Christopher Seward
Lance Shadle
Ernest Shadrick
Steve Shankles
Michael Shannon
Mary Shapiro
Frank Sharum
Rick Shaver
Donell Shaw
Kate Sheaffer
Jeffrey Shelden
Bennie Shelnutt
Kenneth Shelton
Lee Shephard
Andrew Sherman
Judith Sherman
William Sherman
Anthony Shewmake
Chester Shewmake
Larry Shields
Chris Shipley
Bettie Shivey
Lori Shivey
Justin Shoemaker
Amy Shomer
Joi Shoptaw
James Shouse
Vernon Siders, Jr
Janna Sidley
Alan Simmons
Dana Simmons
Linda Simos
Ben Simpson
Jake Simpson
Richard Simpson
Aaron Sims
Hannah Singer
Oliver Sippl
Aubin Siria
Frances Sketoe
Barry Skown
Fred Skowron
David Slade
Scott Slimp
Robert Sloan
Virgil Smart
Perry Smart
Ivan Smith
Mike Smith
Trina Smith
Phillip Smith
Charnette Smith
Hubert Smith
Bryon Smith
William Smith
Randy Smith
Art Smith
Fredrick Smith
Gary Smith
David Smith

Tracy Smith
Chris Smith
Bill Smith
Earl Smith
Larry Smith
Hubert Smith
James Smith
Mark Smith
Glen Smith
Lewis Smith
Ben Snyder
Rick Sobel
Andrea Soligon
Jennifer Solomon
Crystal Son
Carl Soper
Jose Sosa
Victor Sosa
Donato Sotelo
Richard Southworth
Ronny Sowell
Mark Sowell
Guy Spann
Anastasia Spanos
Carl Spears
Brian Spears
Bernard Spencer
David Spicer
Brett Spickard
Tracy Spillman
Nicholas Spiropoulos
Derek Spradlin
George Springer
Jeff Springer
Marcus Springs
William Spurger
Kevin St. John
Shaun Stafford
Peter Stager
Michael Staggers
Greg Stahel
Richard Stalcup
Danny Stalnaker
H.E. Stanley
R.J. Stanley
Joe Stanley
Jerry Stark
Lynda Staton
George Stauber
Zachary Steadman
Michael Stefka
Stephen Steim
Troy Stell
Jim Stephens
Phillip Stephens
Bryan Stevens
Michael Stewart
Mahlon Stewart
Jim Stewart
Amy Stewart
Helen Stewart
Elizabeth Stewart
Kim Stigall
Josh Stinchfield
Ann Stock
Amy Stoltz
Michael Stone
Jason Stone
Jerry Strader
Gwyn Strassle
Stephanie Streett
Kevin Strom
Billy Strope
Tom Strother
Jerry Stroyick
Joe Stroyick
Donnie Sturgeon
John Styron
Wade Sublett
Eyllane Sullivan
James Sullivan
Molly Sullivan

Kevin Sumitt
Tammy Sun
Monica Svojsik
Teresa Swatski
Greg Swayne
John Szczygiel

T

Russell Tacker
Shannon Tanner
Nanik Tanwani
Angel Tapia
Corrine Tapia
Sergio Tarango
Mark Tarnowsky
Stanley Tarnowsky
Billy Tate
Kelly Taylor
Jerry Taylor
Jimmy Taylor
Tim Taylor
Tommy Taylor
Elizabeth Taylor
Jerry Taylor
Brian Taylor
Brad Taylor
James Taylor
Claudia Taylor
Charles Teague
Blythe Teed
Marcus Tenner
Melvin Tenner
Joseph Tennison
Diedre Terai
Jim Terman
Manuel Terrasas
Ronnie Terry
Jim Thacker
Nancy Thaden
J. Thomas Hardin
Randy Thomas
Greg Thomas
Mark Thomason
Daniel Thomason
Aaron Thomason
Chris Thome
Brent Thompson
Alice Thompson
Vernon Thompson
Minnie Thompson
Eric Thomson
Robert Thorne
Phillip Threet
Phil Threet
Fred Threet
Chris Throckmorton
Barbara Thurber
J. Edward Tidwell
Regina Tierney
Scott Tift
Paula Tiller
Mike Tillman
Michael Tillman
Donald Tims
Ed Tinsley
Marietta Tipton
Albert Tipton
Fernando Tiscanero
Juan Tiscareno
Aaron Todd
Nora Toiv
Jason Toland
James Toles
Thomas Tolliver
Eleazar Torres
Ismael Torres
John Torrey
Susan Torricelli
Howard Towler
Todd Townsell
Thomas Townsend
Michael Travelstead

Casey Trawick
Cody Trawick
Freddy Treat
Skye Trimble
Nayan Trivedi
Jon Truelove
Shane Tubbe
Pamela Tubbs
Jerry Tucker
Jimmy Tucker
Tim Tucker
Jeffrey Turback
Michael Turback
Scott Turner
Toney Turner
Samuel Turner, III
Joel Turpin

U

Sandra Udy
Joey Uhiren
Will Umanzor
Clarence Upshaw
Julius Ussery

V

Robby Vale
Carlos Valenzuela
Cassia van der Hoof Holstein
Dennis Vancena
Philip Vanderford
Brian Vanzant
Esequiel Varela
Luis Varela
James Varvel
Carlos Vasquez
Bill Vaughn
Elias Vazquez
Ricardo Vazquez
Evaristo Vega
Ryan Vehr
Juan Velasco
Martin Velasco
Sammy Venable
Kenneth Ventress
Wesley Vick
Billy Victory
Aliber Villanueva
Heriberto Villanueva
Butch Vincent
Alfredo Vincente
Ralph Vines, II
Sara Vitolo
Floyd Vocque
Jon Vollet
George Vollet
Ann Vollet
Laura Vonderhaar

W

Eric Wade
Willie Wade
Mike Wagner
Tracey Walker
Lynn Walker
Jessie Walker
Robert Walkup
Michael Wall
Jack Wallace
Donald Wallace
Dennis Wallace
Jesse Walley
Johnny Walls
Terry Walter
Lawrence Ward
Montell Ward
Tom Ward
Steve Ward
Steven Ward
James Warner
Larry Warner

Gary Washington
James Washington
Rickey Waters
Paul Watkins
Robert Watkins
Andra Watson
Sherman Watson
Steve Watson
Robert Watt
Jeffery Watts
Kellie Watts
Kenneth Watts
Bryan Weaver
Tiffany Weaver
Scott Weaver
Kevin Weaver
Dave Web
Dewayne Webb
Joe Webb
Ronald Webb
Richard Weeks
LeRoy Weibel
Richard Weiss
Jerry Welch
Daniel Welch
Mary Welch
Jon Wellenberger
Jeff Wenaas
Logan West
Charles Wetzler
John Whalen
Joshua Wharton
Robert Whitaker
Derrick White
Allen White
Lance White
Isabel White
Walter Whitebirch
Josh Whited
Harvey Whiteway
Nathan Whitley
Mark Whitson
Robert Wilkerson
Bob Williams
Charlie Williams
Darrion Williams
Danny Williams
David Williams
Edward Williams
Ellis Williams, Jr.
Elmire Williams
Herman Williams
James Williams
Jimmy Williams
Jocke Williams
Matt Williams
Michael Williams
Morris Williams, Jr.
Ronnie Williams
Thomas Williams
Troy Williams
Verneal Williams
Paula Williamson
Bernie Williamson
Mark Williamson
Matt Williamson
Michael Willingham
Jack Willis
Randy Willis
Joyce Willis
Laura Wills
Carl Wilson
Caleb Wilson
George Wilson
Gene Wilson
Joyce Wilson
J Wilson
Rhonda Wilson
Rusty Winemiller
Jerry Wingate
Robert Winkle
Paul Winston

Mikele Winters
Jon Wise
Samuel Withers
Charles Witsell
Joel Wolcott
Amos Wolf
Tom Wolf
S. Bradley Woodall
Bobby Woodard
Kenneth Woodham
Jerry Woodley
Eddie Woods
Ron Woods
Paul Woodson
Tom Woodson
Darrell Woolfolk
Scott Woolridge
Roosevelt Word
Roosevelt Word
Jeffrey Workman
Jordan Worley
Suzanne Worthington
Carol Wrape
Charles Wratten
Jeff Wratten
Robert Wratten
Calvin Wren
Charles Wright
Donald Wright
Fletcher Wright
W. Eric Wright
Dina Wrobleski
Mark Wyatt
Kathy Wyatt
Joyce Wyatt

Y

Geoffery Yamauchi
Elizabeth Yates
Joel Ybarra
W. Randy Yerzyk
Mike Yohanek
Dennis Young
Larry Young
Fred Young
Earl Young
Robert Young
Dan Young
Brien Young
Daniel Young
Doug Younger

Z

Alejandro Zamora
Jimmy Zapata
Jose Zea Mondragon
Francisco Zea Serrano
Nick Zembruski
Troy Zezula
Lenny Zimmermann
Janice Zolin
Richard Zottola

William J. Clinton Presidential Center

The William J. Clinton Presidential Library and Museum

1200 President Clinton Avenue
Little Rock, AR 72201
501-374-4242 tel
www.clintonlibrary.gov

The William J. Clinton Foundation

Choctaw Station
1200 President Clinton Avenue
Little Rock, AR 72201
501-370-8000 tel
www.clintonfoundation.org

The University of Arkansas Clinton School of Public Service

Sturgis Hall, Choctaw Station
1200 President Clinton Avenue
Little Rock, AR 72201
501-683-5200 tel
www.clintonschool.uasys.edu

The Clinton Museum Store

610 President Clinton Avenue
Little Rock, AR 72201
501-748-0400 tel
www.clintonmuseumstore.com

Acknowledgments

The William J. Clinton Presidential Center Building a Bridge to the 21st Century

Project and editorial direction
Melanie Ide

Edited and designed by
Christiaan Kuypers

Project management
Lori Stein

Content guidance
Mary Beth Byrne

Essays writer
Peter Kaminsky

Prepress production
Andrij Borys

Printing
Lowe-Martin/Typogram

This book tells the story of the creation of the William J. Clinton Presidential Center but is also an account of President Clinton's years in office and the work of his administration, as told in the Library's exhibits. Therefore, in addition to acknowledging those who worked on the book, we want to thank those involved in the development of the exhibits from which material was drawn. First and foremost we must thank President Clinton for his participation and reviews. We have been fortunate to have worked with the William J. Clinton Foundation, and give special thanks to Bruce Lindsey, Stephanie Streett, Connie Fails, Debbie Shock, and Jonathan Semans for their ongoing involvement during the creation of both the Library and this book. We thank those of President Clinton's and First Lady Hillary Rodham Clinton's former White House staff who constituted the Exhibit Content Directors Committees; Ted Widmer and West Wing Writers, who wrote much of the exhibit text; and White House photographers Ralph Alswang, Molly Bingham, Sharon Farmer, Phil Humnicky, Barbara Kinney, Robert McNeely, David Scull, Callie Shell, and William Vasta whose many

images appear in these pages and in the exhibits. We also want thank Dr. David Alsobrook, Emily Robison, and all of the archivists, curators, and registrars at the National Archives and Records Administration who provided us with information, access, and insight into the materials of the archives for the exhibit, and John Keller, Stephen Charla, Racheal Carter, and Adam Bergeld who worked on the book. We appreciate the help we received from George Campbell, Courtney O'Donnell, Sasha Blaes, Michelle Stein and Dean Skip Rutherford, and we thank Leslie Garisto, Lois Turel, Joanne Lamb Hayes, and Deena Stein for their editorial assistance and our friends at the office of Polshek Partnership and Hargreaves Associates for their reflections on the project. Finally, President Clinton and the Foundation have asked us to gratefully acknowledge the work of the hundreds of volunteers who continue to joyfully give their time, energy, and spirit to the Clinton Center.

Melanie Ide and Ralph Appelbaum
RAA Editions

Photo Credits

Principal Photography
Timothy Hursley
Benjamin Krain
Nancy Nolan

All photographs courtesy of The William J. Clinton Presidential Library except as noted below:

p.1: ©Timothy Hursley; pp.4-6: ©Timothy Hursley; p.8: ©Yousuf Karsh/Retna Ltd.; p.10: ©Timothy Hursley; p.13: ©Timothy Hursley; p.15: Clinton Global Initiative; pp.16-18: ©Timothy Hursley; p.20: Hargreaves Associates; p.21 top left, top right, bottom right: Hargreaves Associates; bottom left: ©Benjamin Krain; p.23: ©Timothy Hursley; p.24-26: ©Timothy Hursley; p.28: Polshek Partnership; p.29-35: ©Timothy Hursley; p.36: ©Benjamin Krain; p.38: Ralph Appelbaum

Associates; p.39: ©Timothy Hursley; p.41 left: ©Albert Vecerka/Esto; right: ©Benjamin Krain; p.42 left: AP/Stephan Savoia; pp.42-43: ©PF Bentley/pfpix.com; p.43 right: ©Arkansas Democrat-Gazette; p.44 left: ©Nancy Nolan Photography; 44 center row top: ©Reuters/Corbis; center row center and bottom and right row top and bottom: ©PF Bentley/pfpix.com; p.45: ©PF Bentley/pfpix.com; p.46 left: ©Getty Images/Time Life Pictures/Cynthia Johnson; p.46-47: ©Joseph Sohm; p.48: ©Albert Vecerka/Esto; p.49 bottom right: ©Benjamin Krain; p 51 ©Corbis; p.53: ©Timothy Hursley; p.54 left to right: ©Reuters/Corbis/Mike Cordwell; ©AP/Rikard Larma; ©AP/Susan Weems; ©AP; Corbis/NASA; ©AP/Alexander Shogin; p.55, far right: ©AP/Jon Eeg; p.56 left to right: ©Corbis/David Butow; ©AP/Javier Boulez; ©VII/James Nachtwey; ©AP/Elise Amendola; ©AP/Karsten Thielker; p.57 far left: ©AP/John Bazemore; third from right: ©Maggie Steber; far right: ©AP/Jerome Delay; p.58 left to right: ©Contact Press

Images/Greg Girard; ©AP/David Longstreath; NASA; ©AP/pool/Vince Bucci; ©Corbis/Peter Turnley; ©VII/Christopher Morris; p.59 far right: ©AP/Charles Tasnadi; p.60, left to right: ©AP/Dave Martin; ©AP/Elaine Thompson; ©AP/Alexander Zemlianichenko; ©AP/Joe Levy; ©Corbis/Charlotte Observer/J. Siner; p.61 far left: ©AP/Michael Probst; second from left: AP/Kathy Willens; far right: ©AP/Burhan Ozbilici; p.62 left to right: ©AP/Max Nash; ©AP/Luca Bruno; ©AP/Katsumi Kasahara; ©AP/Kevin West; ©AP/JPL; pp.62-63: ©The Boston Herald/Brian Walski; p.63 far left: AP/Chuck Robinson 2nd from right: ©Polaris/AFP/Kemal Jufri; far right: ©AP/John Moore; p.64 left to right: ©AP/Paul Hana; ©AP/Max Nash; ©Getty Images/Time Life Pictures/Herbert Gehr; ©AP/Khalil Senosi; ©Corbis/Steve Liss; p.65 far right: ©AP/Victor R. Caivano; p.66 left to right: ©VII/James Nachtwey; ©Polaris/The Rocky Mountain News/George Kochaniek; ©Corbis/Matt Stone; ©APL/Laurent Reborus; ©Contact

Press Images/Stephen Dupont; p.67 4th from right: ©Getty Images/AFP/Eduardo Verdugo; far right: ©AP/Gregory Bull; p.68 left to right: ©AP/Pool/Gabriel Bouys; ©AP/Elise Amendola; ©AP/World Wide Photos/Toshihiko Sato; ©AP/John Stillwell/WPA Pool; ©AP/U.S. Navy; p.69: 2nd from left: ©Corbis/Paul A. Souders; far right: ©AP/Alan Diaz; p.70 5W Mignon Media-5W Infographics; p.72 5W Mignon Media-5W Infographics ; p.74: ©Albert Vecerka/Esto; p.75: ©Timothy Hursley except for top row left and center row right: ©Albert Vecerka/Esto; p.76 left and bottom right: ©Nancy Nolan Photography; p.77 left: ©Albert Vecerka/Esto; p.78 right: ©Timothy Hursley; p.80 top left: ©AP/Paul Sakuma; bottom left: ©Getty Images/Jean-Marc Giboux/Liason; pp.80-81: ©Timothy Hursley; center right: ©Nancy Nolan Photography; p.83: ©Nancy Nolan Photography; p.84: ©Timothy Hursley; p.85 center right: ©AP/Las Vegas Review-Journal/Amy Beth Bennett; p.85 bottom: Jeff Mankie/Associated Press; p.86: ©Timothy

Hursley; p.87 bottom right: ©Nancy Nolan Photography; p.88 bottom: ©AP/David Longstreath; pp.88-89: ©Timothy Hursley; p.90: ©Nancy Nolan Photography; p.92 bottom left: ©AP/Gary Sussman; pp.92-93: ©Timothy Hursley; pp.94-95 ©Nancy Nolan Photography; p.96: ©Timothy Hursley; p.97 top left: AP/Katsumi Kasahara; top right, bottom left: ©Muench Photography Inc.; p.98 top left: ©Katherine Lambert/Men's Journal, Sept. 2001; bottom left: ©Nancy Nolan Photography; pp.98-99: ©Timothy Hursley; p.100: ©Albert Vecerka/Esto; p.101 top right: ©Corbis/Lewis Alan; p.103 left: ©Nancy Nolan Photography; 104 left: Corbis/Lewis Alan 105 right: ©Nancy Nolan Photography; pp.106-107: ©Albert Vecerka/Esto; p.107 center right: ©Nancy Nolan Photography; p.108 left: ©Nancy Nolan Photography; p.110-111: ©Timothy Hursley; p.111 top left: ©Polaris/AFP/Kemal Jufri; top right: ©Corbis/Caroline Penn; bottom right: ©AP/Aman Sharma; pp.112-113: ©Timothy Hursley 113 right: Nancy

Nolan Photography; p.114 left: ©John Bigelow Taylor; p.115 right: ©John Bigelow Taylor; p.116: ©Corbis/Wally McNamee; p.121 top left, bottom left: ©Arkansas Gazette; p.124 top left: ©Timothy Hursley; p.127 left: ©Nancy Nolan Photography; p.128-129: ©Nancy Nolan Photography; p.132 top left: ©Timothy Hursley right: ©Nancy Nolan Photography; p, 133: ©Nancy Nolan Photography; p.134 top right: ©Timothy Hursley; p.137: ©Nancy Nolan Photography; p.139: ©Timothy Hursley; pp.142-143: ©Albert Vecerka/Esto; p.144: ©Benjamin Krain; p.146: ©PF Bentley/pfpix.com; p.147: ©Benjamin Krain; p.148: ©Nancy Nolan Photography; p.149: ©Benjamin Krain; pp.150-151: ©Timothy Hursley; p.152: Ralph Alswang/Clinton Foundation; p.155: Clinton Global Initiative; p.156: top left: Clinton Global Initiative; top right Ralph Alswang/Clinton Foundation; bottom left: Sasha Blaes, Clinton Foundation; pp.158-159: ©Nancy Nolan Photography; p.162 left: ©Clinton Birthplace Foundation; p.167: Willie Allen